REALISING HOPE

REALISING HOPE

ANDREW PETERS

REALISING HOPE
First Edition published 2007 as *Breaching Negativity*
Second Edition published 2015

© Andrew Peters 2015

Published by A.E. & L.A. Peters Outreach Enterprises
PO Box 225, Mansfield LPO. QLD Australia 4122
Website: www.outreachenterprises.com.au

Scripture quotations from the following version:

RSV: [Scripture quotations are] from the Revised Standard Version of the Bible, copyright © 1946, 1952, and 1971 the Division of Christian Education of the National Council of the Churches of Christ in the United States of America. Used by permission. All rights reserved.

NASB: "Scripture taken from the NEW AMERICAN STANDARD BIBLE®, Copyright © 1960,1962,1963,1968,1971,1972,1973,1975,1977,1995 by The Lockman Foundation. Used by permission.

NKJV: "Scripture taken from the New King James Version®. Copyright © 1982 by Thomas Nelson, Inc. Used by permission. All rights reserved."

NLT: Holy Bible. New Living Translation copyright© 1996, 2004, 2007 by Tyndale House Foundation. Used by permission of **Tyndale House Publishers Inc.**, Carol Stream, Illinois 60188. All rights reserved

National Library of Australia Cataloguing-in-Publication entry
    Peters, Andrew E., author.
    Realising Hope / Andrew E. Peters.
    ISBN: (paperback) 978-0-9923637-2-7 (paperback)
    Subjects: Bible. Romans.
            Negativity (Philosophy)
            Negativism
            Self-realization
            Christian Life—Biblical teaching
    Dewey Number: 158.1

TABLE OF CONTENTS

CHAPTER ONE

INTRODUCTION

This book sets out to assist all men, women and children to engage the circumstances of everyday life, and turn them into opportunities for growth in perseverance, character and hope. The pitfalls of negativity assail all of us, no matter our gender, cultural background or circumstances. Success comes from the utilization of those opportunities, not simply from extra special breaks or circumstances. Many of those who have been successful in life have done so by overcoming great difficulties and troubles to gain those achievements. Life's circumstances call us as individual persons, made in the likeness and image of the Living God, to make a decision as to what we will do or not do with those circumstances.

Will we let life's trials, tribulations and difficulties weigh us down, or will we use them to become the best person that we can be, to attain our full potential? I remember in college many years ago, having a visit from a dental student. He was down in the dumps in a big way. As he poured out woe upon woe about how hard things were and how unmotivated he felt, I jumped to my feet and did something I had never done before or since: I ordered him to get up out of the mud pool and go and do his work and pass his exams. In shock he rose and left my room. A couple of weeks later, at breakfast, he said to me across the table "thanks." He had got up out of the mud pool, studied and passed his exams.

What circumstances have got under your skin that make you feel unable to cope and weighed down under life's trials?

Whatever they may be this book aims to help you understand the place of trials, tribulations and difficulties in God's purpose for your life. It will give you principles to apply to the situations that confront you and enable you to rise above them and use them to do great things for God and His Kingdom.

In the early part of this book I focus on the impact of negativity in our lives because it stands as one of the foremost enemies of hope – a hope that will prevail, a hope that will be realised. Moltmann notes that *realism* teaches us a sense of reality – "for what is"; whereas *hope* awakens a sense of possibility or potential in us – "for what could be".[1] Realism and concrete action relate to using what is, what exists now, whereas hope looks towards something in the future, to something that does not yet exist. However, the realisation of hope can only occur when we successfully link the present to the future. A hope that does not connect successfully with the present only produces *utopias* or *pie-in-the-sky ideas* that rarely, if ever, happen. Moltmann writes:

> If our actions were directed only to the future, we should fall victim to utopias; if they were related only to the present, we should miss our chances.[2]

By linking the future with the present we move to use our current resources, meagre as they may be, to begin to realise a future hope, that is, "we link far-off goals with goals within reach".[3] That is, we do what we can in the present that makes

---

[1] Jürgen Moltmann, Ethics of Hope, trans., Margaret Kohl (London: SCM Press, 2012), 3.

[2] Moltmann, 3.

[3] Moltmann, 3.

our hopes for the future take shape and begin to happen – impossible as those hopes might seem.

We applied this process in our Parish at Everton Park in regard to building a new church. The project was deemed a *pie-in-the-sky* idea by our distractors that would never happen. It was linked with an extremely difficult contextual problem with a sewerage utility that we were told would never be installed.[4] In addition, we lost forty percent of our congregation before the actual building of the new church began to take shape. The sewage utility was finally completed in September 2013 (after 17 years of effort to make it happen) and the church dedicated on 15th December 2013. Early in 2008 our Parish Council (Church Board), utilized a *one-step-at-a time* process. We looked at what we could do in the present that might one day see a real church built on our property.

We used the meagre resources we had on hand to build a new alfresco patio for the new church. It was the first step in a whole line of individual steps that finally saw the realisation of our dreams – a contemporary church that could impact new generations with the Gospel of Jesus Christ. It took some time before the local community could recognise the new building as a church. However, the new lighted cross and sign installed on the building before Christmas 2014 removed all doubts and placed the new church as a beacon on a hill. I can assure you that negativity worked really hard to stall this project and stop it dead in its tracks.

---

[4] To connect with the BCC/QUU sewer system we had to install a 250 metre sewer main that went through six properties, with nine manholes, and the entire project being done through a watercourse.

However, what developed through those troubles, difficulties and trials was a church community who knew how to persevere and develop character in troubled times. You can be sure of one thing: negativity wants you overwhelmed in the present so you can make no or little impact on the future. So it is time to do it in – to overcome negativity and produce a hope that will not disappoint, a hope that will be realised (Romans 5:5).

NEGATIVITY'S ASSAULT ON OUR LIVES

Negativity may come initially as an uninvited guest into our lives. However, when we do not dismiss its provoking thoughts and ideas, and allow those thoughts and ideas to park themselves and fester in our minds and hearts, then negativity begins to take possession of us. We find ourselves not only expressing those very thoughts and ideas, but believing them as well. Negativity can come upon us quickly, overwhelm us and leave us devastated in its wake; or it can gradually seep into our lives and gradually take over the way we think, feel and act. Negativity can arise out of the frustrations of life that create a feeling of hopelessness and despair, until we feel that we can never win or get ahead. It can also gain access into our lives through the type of people we mix with as friends and companions. Who do you listen to in your life? Whose ideas and thoughts sway your very actions and attitudes? We choose the voices that we allow to speak into our live - the voices that influence the way we look, believe and behave.

Check it out. Are your friends and companions encouraging people who help you stretch and grow, so you can reach your full potential? Or are they critical, cynical and self-absorbed people who always rubbish those who at least are having a go at doing something? Do those who speak into your life encourage you to aim for the best, to do things as excellently as you can,[5] or are they those who say near enough is good enough?[6] What type of people surround you in your life, what type of people do you gravitate to in a crowd, or at church? For many years I worked in Kings Cross with Teen Challenge, reaching out to broken and hurt young people who were destroying their lives. One day I realized that all the people in my life were either broken and needy people; or they were like me, those who worked continuously with broken and needy people. I decided I needed friends who did not need me to be their counsellor, rescuer or mentor. I needed people who were alive and going somewhere so they could challenge me to go for it. I went looking for them and found them.

Negativity moves into our lives to rob us of the intimacy of our relationship with God. It not only creates a shadow over all that God has promised to us through Jesus, but robs us of what God has already given to us. It aims to disintegrate the life giving promises of Jesus in our lives. It seeks to rob us of the abundant life that Jesus promised to us, and the joy of serving God with all our might. Negativity seeks to create fear and uncertainty in the area of our destiny and purpose and produce the corrosive elements of cynicism in the things that we do. Negativity tugs at our resiliency to changing times and

---

[5] Excellence in all that we do is not the achievement of perfection, but doing the best you possibly can with the resources you have available.

[6] Have you ever thought of people you hope would never treat life as "near enough is good enough"? Do we want our brain surgeon saying, well I think that is near enough, let sow him up!"

seduces us to move against the work of God and those who faithfully serve Him, by murmuring and groaning. It instigates inflexibility and intolerance in our hearts and impacts the relationships we have with others. Negativity selects our friends for us and drives us away from the life-giving presence of positive men and women of God.

NEGATIVITY GIVES A SENSE OF BEING LEFT BEHIND

One of the surest lies that negativity brings into our hearts and minds is that life has left us behind and that we can never succeed or do well with the little that we have. Proverbs 13:23 (NASB) notes that:

Abundant food is found in the fallow ground of the poor

This verse indicates that even the poorest person on the face of the planet has the potential for abundant return on the very ground upon which he or she stands. God has made a provision for you, in the skills and abilities that He gave to you, meagre though they may seem to you, so that you may prosper and succeed in the important things of life. He intends for you to prosper in the things that pertain to eternity and the things that last far beyond the destroying and disintegrating forces at work around you.

God sent His Son Jesus Christ into the world to shatter the chains and barriers that hold us back from reaching our full potential. Through His death on the cross and resurrection from the dead, Jesus Christ has given us the potential to enter into an eternal love relationship with God. Through Jesus we have been invited into the eternal communion or fellowship of God the Father, the Son and the Holy Spirit. It is not simply an adoption into the family of God, but an invitation into their love and intimacy.

However, Proverbs 13:23 also resounds with a chilling reminder that the very promise of provision and productivity given to every man, woman and child on the planet is also assailed by negative forces when it cries out:

But it is swept away by injustice.

This phrase suggests that unjust business and political forces can rob the poor of their rightful fruit for the hard work they do. It speaks against systemic and structural evil that prevents the poor of having a just legal and political system to redress the oppression that often comes upon them.[7] Thus the negative person will complain bitterly about the abuse of the political or legal system, or even more destructive, against those who seem to have succeeded because they have had better circumstances. This is not to say that some of the complaints are not valid, but raises the question of how the poor can realise the hope of prosperity that their fallow ground can provide, despite injustice.

The real evil hinted at in this verse is the impact of injustice that produces in the poor a *loss of hope.* That is, a loss of the type of hope that does not disappoint. In other words what is really lost is *expectation* - the expectation that appropriate effort will produce the desired results and bring about prosperity. There is an adoption of an internal mindset of

---

[7] Daniel Treier, *Proverbs & Ecclesiastes* (Grand Rapids, MI: Brazos Press, 2011), 90-91. We have seen enough regarding oppression elsewhere to realize that Proverbs takes note of systemic sin and structural evil.

defeat, which was initially caused by external forces, but now resides in the heart of the poor, not just their external circumstances. Now, whilst we agree that systemic and structural evil makes the going hard, railing against the unfairness of things does not assist in gaining prosperity. When we explore the meaning of this verse again,

Abundant food is found in the fallow ground of the poor
But it is swept away by injustice

we find that the impact of injustice is to produce a half-hearted effort (not no effort) by the poor to capitalise upon the very ground that they possess. This is noted by the fact that the ground of the poor, which can produce abundant food, remains *fallow*.

The fact that the ground is fallow means that the poor here are not seen as lazy or slothful. In farming terms, *fallow ground* is ground that has been ploughed, but *not yet sown with seed*. This statement ensures that we do not write off the poor as just being too lazy or slothful to do the work necessary to prosper. The initial and hard work of ploughing and preparing the ground for sowing has been done. However, the work is not finished, because the seed has not been sown. Without the seed there is no harvest and without a harvest the *impossibility* of prosperity becomes more extreme.

Now even though Proverbs does not portray the poor as lazy or slothful in this verse, they still battle the forces that can push them into such laziness or slothfulness. These forces produce two things: first, is a lack of caring for, or indifference to, one's responsibilities; and the second is despair at the possibility of salvation – the movement to extreme hopelessness.[8] That is, it breaches the expectation that even in the toughest of circumstances God can help us break through, overcome and prosper. It exaggerates the difficulties of the circumstances and hides (cloaks them so they become invisible) the potential and possibilities resident in those circumstances. This makes it hard for the poor to capitalise upon the ground that they have been given and use the resources they already have. Even though the difficulties encountered by the poor began with external barriers, they are now robbed internally of their prosperity, because they can no longer see the potential that lies in the fallow ground at their feet. They can no longer see their own potential. The solution does only not lie in an improvement in their external circumstances, but in a change of heart. Success does not begin outside but inside.

---

[8] Treier, 90-91. Beyond this, the Christian tradition defines sloth much more broadly than laziness: "The sins of sloth has two components: *acedial*, which means a lack of caring, an aimless indifference to one's responsibilities to God and to man, and *tristitia*, meaning sadness and sorrow. In its final stages sloth becomes despair at the possibility of salvation." Certainly in Proverbs refusal to work can be recognized as problematic in secular terms. However, the larger issue is refusal to undergo with hope the godly discipline, including work that fosters wisdom."

CHAPTER TWO
NEGATIVITY IS A SOUL ISSUE

Negativity is a soul issue. As such negativity influences and impacts the thinking, feeling and decision making centre of our being.[1] It relates to the dysfunctional attempts of the soul to deal with everyday discouragements and setbacks. The soul's perspective becomes dysfunctional because it relegates those discouragements and setbacks to external forces, rather than seeing the soul's potential to overcome those difficulties and prosper anyway. In his third letter, John notes that our health and external prosperity are directly linked to the internal prosperity of our souls. He says,

> Beloved I pray that in all respects you may prosper and be in good health, just as your soul prospers.[2]

It is the *just* that makes all the difference. People often believe that external success is dependent upon external breaks or circumstances. Thus the negative person will belittle those who are successful and prosperous because he or she never seems to get the same type of breaks or opportunities. Yet opportunities come to each of us at different times and in different places. Brian Houston notes that time and chance happen to us all where,

---

[1] In the three-fold understanding of the human person, the soul is the decision making centre of the human person which responds positively to the quiet still voice of the Holy Spirit, speaking through our own spirit, or listens to the pounding clamour of the desires of the world and the lusts of the flesh that operate through our body, with its senses and drives. See *Holiness without the Law* by Andrew Peters.

[2] 3 John 2 (NASB).

TIME refers to that moment in life when you stand on the edge of your CHANCE or opportunity at destiny...you are about to collide with your life's purpose.[3]

Those who have overcome the debilitating impact of negativity find that opportunities lie all around them and they endeavour to make those opportunities work for them rather than against them. They also gain the capability of making negative circumstances work in their favour, so that over the long haul they come out on top.

For example, when we were pastors in the country town of Ballan in Victoria, the local Shire Council asked me to represent the Shire on the regional "Poor Box" committee. The Poor Box was run by the magistrate's court. Before the advent of speed cameras, if you had been found guilty of a speeding charge, the magistrate had the option of fining you or ordering you to put money in the poor box. A contribution to the poor box would be around $100. The money from the poor box would then be distributed to the poor. As the only resident minister in our country town, I thought some additional funding would definitely help to meet the needs of the poor people who came to me for emergency relief. When I arrived at the magistrate's court in Geelong, I discovered that there were many others thinking the same way, as the court room was packed with people from other caring groups, also wanting funding for the needs of the poor.

The magistrate called for order and within a short time informed us all that though there was a pie it was very much reduced in size since the last time the committee had met.

---

[3] Brian Houston, *Get a Life* (Sydney: Hillsong, 1996), 10-11.

This was due to the impact of the speed camera system of fining. The extent of the reduction was not immediately known and it was moved that we adjourn for a month, return and then split up the pie among the various groups wanting funding. A month later I arrived back in the courtroom. When I arrived the courtroom was empty, apart from the magistrate and his two assistants. As I was early I thought the others would be here soon. Come the time of the meeting, I was still the only person sitting in the courtroom, apart from the magistrate and his two assistants. At that point the magistrate looked up from what he was doing and realized I was there. He said, "Oh, you haven't heard." That is never good news. It seems that during the interceding month all the other groups had rung the magistrate and managed to get their piece of the pie and there was none left.

I felt a bit naive at that point - new at this game. I hadn't known how the game was played; otherwise I would have called too and acquired whatever meagre amount I could have got as our part of the pie. As I got up to leave, saying farewell to the magistrate, he asked me where I came from. When I told him he suggested I wait a minute, whilst he checked with the magistrate in Ballarat, a city near our country church. He came back and told me that the other magistrate could help me with something - small that it might be. I contacted the other magistrate and received an initial amount of $600 to help, with instructions to ring back when I had used that amount to see whether they had any more. For TEN YEARS the Ballarat magistrate's court in that country city provided enough funding for us to meet all the emergency relief needs that came to us in that time.

DISCUSSION/REFLECTION QUESTIONS:

1. What type of thoughts lead to a negative attitude?

2. What type of people or professionals do you sincerely hope do not follow the philosophy: "Near enough is good enough"?

3. List some types of comments that indicate someone is belittling your ability to do anything extraordinary.

4. List some types of comments that indicate someone is encouraging you to go for the best that you can be.

5. What thoughts or ideas prevent people using the skills, abilities and opportunities that they have?

6. How has Jesus released you or people you know from the impact of negative thoughts and ideas?

7. Do you think the saying; "every cloud has a silver lining" is true for every discouraging situation or set-back? Why?

8. Are there opportunities that you have missed because you blamed circumstances for a lack of prosperity or fruitless-ness? Give an example.

9. The soul is made up of our emotions (attitudes and feelings), mind and will. How can people change their attitudes, thinking or decision-making processes that will result in transforming their troubles or difficult situations turning into something good, prosperous or fruitful.?

10. Have you ever been naive, stupid or silly in a situation? What could you have done in that situation to come out on top?

11. Pick one thing that is in your power to change right now that will improve things for you in a week, month or year's time? What do you need to do to implement that change?

12. In your daily life, what type of people do you spend time with? Do they uplift you and encourage you to achieve or try new things? Do they discourage you from doing anything beyond the norm?

CHAPTER THREE
NEGATIVITY'S INTERNAL NATURE

Negativity diminishes our capability to see opportunities when they arise and to capitalize on those opportunities when we do see them. Because negativity is more concerned with self-centeredness or self-absorption than either God or others, it never rises above the level of mediocrity to take on the challenge of beating the odds and overcoming the impossibilities. Negativity is an internal response to external troubles, disappointments and failure. Negativity tends to blame external circumstances rather than to look at the soul's own response to the issues of life. Negativity reflects people who have allowed soul-defeating influences to infiltrate their inner heart and bring him or her down.[1] Proverbs warns us to:

> Watch over your heart with all diligence, for from it flows the springs of life.[2]

Negativity robs us of an inner resiliency to changing times and new challenges and takes away the vibrancy of life.[3] Negativity takes away from the "Christian" person the abundant life, peace and joy that Jesus has given to him or her. Note that it takes away what has already been given, not simply that which had been promised. Negative people turn

---

[1] Houston, 29-30. Brian Houston notes, "The church is often a target for negativity but I believe that IN EVERY CIRCUMSTANCE negativity is not about any of these things. It is about YOU.

[2] Proverbs 4:23 (NASB).

[3] George Parsons and Speed B. Leas, *Understanding Your Congregation as a System* (New York: Alban Institute Publications, 1994), 3.

the Word of God around to question why God has not fulfilled what He has promised, when they have not used what He has already given to them. They have not developed or nurtured the promises of God within themselves. John notes that our ability to overcome external difficulties and forces arises from the presence of Jesus within us "because greater is He who is in you than he who is in the world."[4] Brian Houston notes that

> Negative people draw on negative experiences and build their beliefs and opinions around them. Then they justify their position because of what has happened to them.[5]

Those experiences are certainly real, for many people have suffered incredible abuse and atrocities in their lives. None of us are exempt from the experience of overwhelming circumstances and situations. However, those experiences should not continue to be the foundation upon which we build our life, or rather the foundation upon which we disintegrate our future. Positive people, on the other hand may have suffered in similar ways, but they have, through Jesus, moved beyond those experiences and have broken through. They have become "committed to changing themselves to line up with the Word of God," rather than changing the Word of God to meet their circumstances.[6]

NEGATIVITY IS THE SOUL'S RESISTANCE TO GOD'S PROCESSES

Negativity arises in people's lives because of a process that they go through which is meant to develop in them

---

[4] 1 John 4:4 (NASB).

[5] Houston, 35.

[6] Houston, 35.

perseverance, character, and hope. It arises because of their dysfunctional response to the difficulties, troubles and problems of life. According to Jesus, negativity develops in a person's soul because of his or her response to three different external sources. In the parable of the sower Jesus noted three types of people who fail to bear fruit for the Kingdom of God:

1. People who listen to wrong voices;
2. People who succumb to persecution and tribulation;
3. People who are overwhelmed by anxiety over the basic provisions for everyday life; and

and one type of person that does bear fruit:

4. People who listen to the word God has given to them; ponders upon it and then acts on the word they have been given.

1. *People who listen to wrong voices:* people develop negativity because they listen to wrong voices in their lives. Jesus said,

> When any one hears the word of the kingdom and does not understand it, the evil one comes and snatches away what is sown in his heart.[7]

The word "understand" does not simply mean to make sense of something, but refers to a process of thinking through and reflecting upon a matter, to understand its meaning. People choose the voices they listen to and take notice of in their lives. Because of that, they often do not take the time and effort to think seriously through what God is saying to them.

---

[7] Matthew 13:19 (NASB).

They are just too busy attempting to fulfil all the other demands in their life.

In the temptation story Jesus shows us both the identity and character of the enemy who speaks into our lives. This enemy has one desire: to rob us of the vibrant life and prosperity that God wants us to enjoy.[8] His identity is Satan (i.e., the devil), and his character is one of deceiver and liar. He manages to snatch God's word from us by convincing us that we can think about it later, when things are more settled. He attempts to convince us that what God has to say is neither urgent nor important. However, when things do settle down, we no longer have the word to reflect upon.

On another occasion Jesus said to the Jews listening to Him,

> You are of your father the devil, and you want to do the desires of your father. He was a murderer from the beginning, and does not stand in the truth, because there is no truth in him. Whenever he speaks a lie, he speaks from his own nature, for he is a liar, and the father of lies.[9]

They as leaders of the people of God had moved away from God and what He had been saying to them. They had begun to listen to another voice - the voice of one who primarily wanted to rob them of their Godly heritage, destroy them as nation and annihilate them altogether. Whereas Jesus had come to restore their Godly heritage, rebuild them as a nation and give them eternal life. Jesus said,

> The thief comes only to steal and kill and destroy; I came that they may have life, and have it abundantly.[10]

---

[8] Matthew 4.
[9] John 8:44 (NASB).
[10] John 10:10 (NASB).

They continued to listen to "another" voice. It cost them their nation, their city and their Temple, as in 70 A.D. the Roman army destroyed it all before them. Meanwhile the Church that Jesus instigated went on to defeat the Roman Empire in 315 A.D, with the conversion of the Emperor Constantine, without a sword being drawn.

2. ***People who succumb to persecution and tribulation:*** people who harbour negativity in their hearts lack the inner resiliency to changing times and the ability to meet the new challenges they bring.[11] They find it difficult to be strong and supple in times of tribulation and trouble. Jesus said,

> As for what was sown on rocky ground, this is he who hears the word and immediately receives it with joy; yet he has no root in himself, but endures for a while, and when tribulation or persecution arises on account of the word, immediately he falls away.[12]

Persecution arises in a variety of forms and guises. It can range from threatening our privileges and reputation to threatening our lives. It can arise simply because we belong to Christ or because we stand by God's principles and ways. Negativity robs people of their backbone to stand by God and what He says, no matter what the circumstances might say or do. Negativity fuels the fires of fear within us and drives us to a sense of self-preservation and selfishness that robs us of everything that God wants to give to us through Jesus Christ.

---

[11] Andrew Peters, *The Emerging Paradigm of Diversity* (Mansfield, QLD: A.E. & L.A. Peters Outreach Enterprises, 2011).

[12] Matthew 13:20-21 (NASB).

3. **People who are overwhelmed by anxiety over the basic provisions for everyday life:** people gravitate to negativity because of an anxiety over the provision of basic everyday things that enable us to survive in this world. Jesus said,

> And others are the ones sown among thorns; they are those who hear the word, but the cares of the world, and the delight in riches, and the desire for other things, enter in and choke the word, and it proves unfruitful.[13]

This desire for riches and other things does not guarantee that they actually manage to acquire those things. Usually it means they don't, no matter how much they hanker after them. Subsequently, negativity expresses itself as a criticism of those who have become successful and prosperous in life. People can find very good religious reasons for denying others the honor of their achievements and the fruit for their efforts. The ones they really rob are themselves. Christians who engage themselves in the fruitless desire for the riches of this world, or who become anxious about the cares of this world, have failed to understand the real source of prosperity in our life and the provision of the things we need to survive in this world. Jesus said,

> But seek first his kingdom and his righteousness, and all these things shall be yours as well. Therefore do not be anxious about tomorrow, for tomorrow will be anxious for itself. Let the day's own trouble be sufficient for the day.[14]

God does not desire to deprive us of the basic provisions of everyday life, nor does He frown upon our being prosperous

---

[13] Mark 4:18-19 (RSV).
[14] Matthew 6:33-34 (RSV).

in the things of this world. His primary concern is our attempt to gain those provisions or possess prosperity independent of Him. As our Heavenly Father He desires to provide our basic necessities as well as to prosper us in the things that we do.

4. **Positive people bear fruit:** positive people choose carefully the people they listen to in their lives and the people who have influence in their decision making processes. They listen for God's voice and when they hear the Word of God they take time to listen and understand what God is saying to them. Jesus said,

   > As for what was sown on good soil, this is he who hears the word and understands it; he indeed bears fruit, and yields, in one case a hundredfold, in another sixty, and in another thirty.[15]

Because they take time out to understand what God is trying to say to them, they begin to draw upon the life-giving power that comes to us through the Word of God and the working of the Holy Spirit. They allow the Word of God to infiltrate their souls and transform their perceptions of the world and the purpose and will of God. They no longer conform to the ways and thoughts of this world but are transformed by the renewal of their minds. They no longer seek to please the world and its agenda but seek to do that which is pleasing to God.[16]

God's desire for His people is not only to have abundant life, but to be prosperous in all they do. The Psalmist begins his book by noting that the person, who turns away from the

---

[15] Matthew 13:23 (RSV).

[16] Romans 12:1-2.

31

debilitating impact of negativity, will prosper in whatever he or she does.[17] The Psalmist notes three aspects of negativity that we need to turn away from in order to sow seeds of prosperity in our lives:

1. *Do not walk in the counsel of the wicked.* This means we are not to take the advice of the wicked and be lured down the same path they take, which only leads to destruction. Proverbs tells us neither to be enticed by sinners nor to enter into their form of negativity which abuses the innocent and only leads to evil (Proverbs 1:10ff).

2. *Do not stand in the paths of sinners.* This means that we are not to follow in the paths of those who have forsaken God and His ways and have turned to their own ways of selfishness and self-centredness.

3. *Do not sit in the seat of scoffers.* This means that we are not to enter into the critical perspective of cynicism and pessimism that only sits and criticises what others do and shreds their efforts at building the Kingdom God.

Those who wish to prosper need first to turn away from the things that contribute to negativity, and turn to do those things that contribute to prosperity. The Psalmist also notes that it is God's greatest desire to see His people rise up to prosperity in their lives. He writes,

> The Lord be magnified, who delights in the prosperity of his servant.[18]

---

[17] Psalm 1.

[18] Psalm 35:27 (NASB).

It is not a matter of whether bad things happen to good people, but when bad things do happen to good people how they handle it. Negativity calls us to wallow in self-pity and despair, whereas God calls us to rise above the circumstances and overcome them in and through Jesus Christ. In the Book of Revelation, Jesus' message to each of the seven churches was He would reward "...he who overcomes,"[19] despite the fact that each of them suffered from different external and internal pressures.

DISCUSSION/REFLECTION QUESTIONS:

1. What signs indicate that people are weighed down by troubles and difficulties?

2. What promises has God given to us that enable us to overcome some of the difficulties and troubles that life brings?

3. Contrast the types of advice given which leads to negativity with those which lead to prosperity and fruitfulness?

4. How does God provide for our everyday needs? Give examples.

5. What are the key differences between those who are fruitful and unfruitful in the things they do?

6. Why does sitting in the seat of scoffers negativity in our lives?

7. Why do we doubt that God wants us to prosper? What can we do about it?

---

[19] Revelation 2-3.

CHAPTER FOUR
OVERCOMING NEGATIVITY'S THRUST

In encouraging people to overcome the internal and external pressures they encounter, we do not want to underestimate the impact of those external pressures and circumstances that cause such distress. External pressures, troubles, difficulties and catastrophes influence and affect us in many ways. Sometimes the outward pressures can be extreme to say the least. They may overwhelm us in a moment of time. Often those circumstances have been arranged to gain control over our souls and bring us into captivity. "My soul," David noted in anguish during one period of his life, "is among lions; I must lie among those who breathe forth fire".[1] Again in one of the Psalms of ascent David described the way in which negative circumstances would have completely engulfed them if it had not been for the Lord's help:

> The waters would have engulfed us, the stream would have swept over our soul; then the raging waters would have swept over our soul.[2]

The difficulty is that overwhelming circumstances do enslave us emotionally and spiritually. Our souls can become dismayed, troubled, disturbed, refuse to be comforted, enslaved by fleshly lusts, and imprisoned like a bird in a trap.[3] In Psalms 142 and 143 David describes a process by which his soul suffered torment and oppression.

---

[1] Psalm 57:4 (NASB).

[2] Psalm 124:4-5.

[3] Psalms 6:3; 31:7; 42:5; 77:10; 88:3; 124:7; 1 Peter 2:11.

1. *Outward Negative Circumstances:* the problem began with external persecution. The forces that had come against David and his small group of men were intense and unreasonable. There were those out to bring him down. He tells us that:

   > They have hidden a trap for me;[4] and again,

   > For the enemy has persecuted my soul; he has crushed my life to the ground.[5]

2. *Spirit is Overwhelmed:* this external persecution and attack then had an internal impact on David, whereby his spirit was overwhelmed within him. He cries:

   > Therefore my spirit is overwhelmed within me; My heart is appalled within me.[6]

   "Appalled" is a strong emotive word. David was entirely overcome within himself at what had happened. Not only that but he was at a loss as to why it had happened.

3. *Results:* This brought a number of results in David's life:

   • *Sense of hopelessness and imprisonment* – David felt trapped and caught in an ever increasing nightmare, where there seemed to be no way out. He tells us:

   > For there is no escape for me.[7]

---

[4] Psalm 142:3 (NASB).

[5] Psalm 143:3 (NASB).

[6] Psalms 142:3; 143:4(RSV).

[7] Psalm 142:4 (NASB).

- *Sense of self-pity* – this sense of hopelessness in David caused him to wallow initially in self-pity. Woe is me he cries for no one cares for me. He says:

  For there is no one who regards me...No one cares for my soul.[8]

- *Lack of direction and purpose* – this sense of desertion and self-pity created a listlessness in David and he felt that there is no light to show him the way out, no answer that could be found to resolve the situation

  He has made me dwell in dark places, like those who have long been dead.[9]

Though David was overwhelmed and overcome by negative external forces, as well as negative internal reactions, he didn't remain there. He eventually broke through in God and became King of all Israel. David worked through a threefold process:

- *Remembered the God of His past* – he began to remember and recite the things that God had done for him in the past. When overwhelmed by circumstances outside of our control we need to remember and repeat God's saving acts from the past.

- *Brought that God into the present* – he then recognized that the God of the past was the same God who was on his side in the present circumstances. God had not deserted him and God would come to his aid. We

---

8 Psalm 142:4 (NASB).

9 Psalm 143:3 (NASB).

need to identify God's presence in our current circumstances and call upon His help in the midst of those circumstances and difficulties.

- *So that He could break through with God into the future* - David finally broke through the circumstances that surrounded him, overcame the negative forces they represented and went forward to become King of Israel.[10]

The difficulty with negativity is that it frustrates us in the present so that we do not apply ourselves to the things that need to be done now to break into the future. Brian Houston notes that negativity tends to limit the present and sabotage the future, because it produces limited, powerless thinking that reduces our expectation level, and therefore our future achievement level.[11]

THE FRUIT OF NEGATIVITY

Negativity relates to both the attitudes we carry and the seeds we sow into our lives. Paul writes,

> Do not be deceived, God is not mocked; for whatever a man sows, this he will also reap. For the one who sows to his own flesh shall from the flesh reap corruption, but the one who sows to the Spirit shall from the Spirit reap eternal life.[12]

Negativity grows like weeds, from seeds we have sown in our lives that eventually produce the negative attitudes we express to others. A poor attitude comes from consistently

---

[10] Psalms 143:5-6 (NASB).

[11] Houston, 55.

[12] Galatians 6:7-8 (NASB).

sowing poor seeds into our lives. The farming community has found God's creation to be consistent in what it produces. Seeds only reproduce in kind, unless they have been cross-bred with other seeds. That is, wheat produces wheat, potatoes produce potatoes and corn produces corn. We also find that sheep give birth to lambs and cows give birth to calves. The seed that a farmer plants will determine the crop he will harvest.

The same goes with us. The physical, emotional and spiritual seeds we sow in our lives will produce a harvest, either of corruption and poverty, or righteousness and prosperity. If we sow the wrong seeds in our lives then we are foolish to think that we will bear good fruit. Jesus said,

> For no good tree bears bad fruit, nor again does a bad tree bear good fruit; for each tree is known by its own fruit. For figs are not gathered from thorns, nor are grapes picked from a bramble bush. The good man out of the good treasure of his heart produces good, and the evil man out of his evil treasure produces evil; for out of the abundance of the heart his mouth speaks.[13]

Negativity also tends to diminish the fruit of the good seeds we sow in our lives and enhances the results of the poor seeds. It is why the Pharisees never reaped the harvest of their tithing. They had been meticulous in the area of tithing, but had forgotten some rather important areas of their spiritual life, such as, justice, mercy, faith and the love of God.[14] It is not enough to sow good seeds to produce good fruit; we must also stop sowing bad seeds. Often the bad

---

[13] Luke 6:43-45 (NASB).
[14] Matthew 23:23; Luke 11:42.

seeds we sow grow up as weeds and thorns that overwhelm and suffocate the good seeds we have sown. In the Parable of the Sower Jesus notes, "Other seed fell among thorns and the thorns grew up and choked it, and it yielded no grain."[15] We often do not see the fruit for our effort because we sow mixed seed, and the mixed seeds tend to nullify one another. Brian Houston notes,

> Nothing will negate the Holy Spirit's power in your life quicker than negativity. To negate means to nullify or neutralise, and just as the work of the Holy Spirit points to positives, negativity works against His purpose.[16]

We need to modify and balance what we sow, lest the weeds we sow grow so prolifically that they negate all the good seeds we sow.

DISCUSSION/REFLECTION QUESTIONS:

1. What types of external situations create stress and tension?

2. Have you or someone you know felt totally overwhelmed by external situations?

3. Reflect upon or discuss the following feelings/metaphors and what type of situations would cause these feelings –

   - dismayed,
   - troubled,
   - disturbed,
   - refuse to be comforted,
   - enslaved by fleshly lusts, and
   - imprisoned like a bird in a trap.

---

15 Mark 4:7 (RSV).

16 Houston, 53.

4. What type of things has God done in the past that have helped you or others you know get through difficult situations and troubled times?

5. How could those past actions of God help you or others you noted above understand what God could do in the current difficult situation or troubled time?

6. If you, or others you have noted above, were to break through the current restrictions caused by difficult situations or troubled times, what results might occur for you or them and bring further growth to the Kingdom of God?

7. Negativity stops you doing things in the present that will improve your situation in the future. What things are you or others you noted above not doing because of current difficult situations or troubled times, that will impact on the future? What could you or they do about these things?

8. What mixed seeds might you or others you noted above be sowing that are nullifying the results or fruitfulness of yours or their efforts, and diminishing the effectiveness of what you or they are doing? What seeds could you sow instead?

9. In his message to the seven churches in The Book of Revelations Jesus promises to reward those who "overcome". What do you think overcoming means for you or the others you noted above in the current difficult situations or troubled times?

CHAPTER FIVE
NEGATIVITY AND PERCEPTION

Three stone masons were involved in the building of St. Peter's Cathedral in Rome. A passerby asked the men what they were doing. The first stonemason mumbled that he was chiseling a rock. The second said that he was making a block of stone. But the third stonemason, proclaimed, with a sense of pride, I am helping to build St. Peter's Cathedral. All three men were doing exactly the same work, but each of them had a different perception of what they were doing. Perception makes the difference between being engulfed by negativity or breaking out of the prison of enslaved emotions, thoughts and feelings and overcoming the obstacles that stand in the way of success, prosperity, and fulfilling your destiny in God. The way we see the situations we face often holds us back from solving many of the ongoing problems we encounter that seem to drain our energy and produce a sense of hopelessness.

Two shoe salesmen from competing companies, in the pioneer days, went to Africa to sell shoes. When the first salesmen saw that no one in Africa wore shoes he telegraphed home with a note of despondency and said, "There is no hope of sales here because no one wears shoes." The second salesmen also telegraphed home and said, "Send all the shoes you can, no one has shoes yet".[1] Each faced the same situation, but each of them saw it differently. One saw

---

[1] **http://theoccasionalceo.blogspot.com.au/2010/04/two-shoe- sales-men-rest-of-story.html**. The Occasional CEO, Eric Schultz–2010, April 3.

frustration, the other saw opportunity. The situations we face are more about how we see them, rather than the difficulties we face. [2]

Paul, in his attempt to restore order and balance in the Church he had established at Corinth, tried to help them see how important perception was to the way they saw God working in the midst of their Church. Paul wrote,

> For though we live in the world we are not carrying on a worldly war, for the weapons of our warfare are not worldly but have divine power to destroy strongholds. We destroy arguments and every proud obstacle to the knowledge of God, and take every thought captive to obey Christ. [3]

Paul used three words to describe an ascending development of perception that stands over and against the purposes of God. He notes the movement from argument or speculation (reason); to obstacle or lofty thing; to stronghold or fortress. The following diagram shows this progression:

---

[2] **http://theoccasionalceo.blogspot.com.au/2010/04/two-shoe- sales-men-rest-of-story.html**. The Occasional CEO, Eric Schultz–2010, April 3. This is a true story. The first salesman returned home and accepted another opportunity from his company to work in Paris, where he became successful and very rich. The second salesman stayed in Africa and built an office and warehouse. In the first year he had great difficulty in selling shoes, but persevered and diversified selling sandals, walking sticks, hats and feet lotion, He finally became famous in his adopted country and a millionaire.

[3] 2 Corinthians 10:3-5 (RSV). NRSB Version – "For though we walk in the flesh, we do not war according to the flesh, for the weapons of our warfare are not of the flesh, but divinely powerful for the destruction of fortresses. *We are* destroying speculations and every lofty thing raised up against the knowledge of God, and *we are* taking every thought captive to the obedience of Christ".

```
┌─────────────────────────────────────┐
│  Stronghold or fortress             │
└─────────────────────────────────────┘
                  ⬆
┌─────────────────────────────────────┐
│  Obstacle or lofty thing            │
└─────────────────────────────────────┘
                  ⬆
┌─────────────────────────────────────┐
│  Argument or speculation            │
└─────────────────────────────────────┘
```

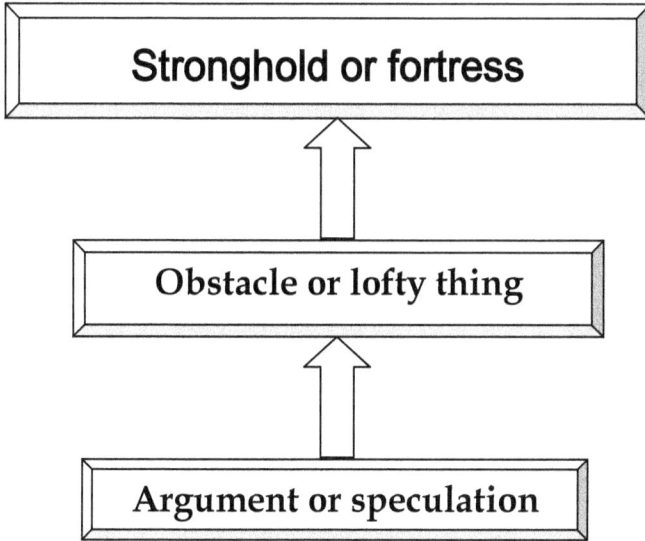

The weapons of warfare, noted by Paul here, are not worldly but divine or spiritual, because the nature of the strongholds or fortresses themselves contains significant spiritual attributes. They are places of entrenchment in thought and activity, whereby people resist all types of godly reproof and instruction that contradicts or challenges those thoughts and activities. This includes both biblical instruction and the wise counsel of anointed men and women of God. These strongholds can be philosophical or theological positions strongly argued for with great eloquence or persuasive speech. They can be, on the one hand, demonic spiritual strongholds that resist and oppose truth, or on the other hand, human error and sin.[4]

---

[4] Ralph Martin, *2 Corinthians*, ed. David Hubbard, Glenn Barker, and Ralph Martin, Word Biblical Commentary (Milton Keynes: Word Publishing, 1986, 1991), 305. 1991 1991 1991 The word is used by both Philo and Paul with this inference.

"Argument" or "speculation" is used here by Paul to note the exultation of *reason*, which has become arrogant in its application, as well as in its perception of the knowledge of God and His truth.[5] A similar exultation of reason arose from the Enlightenment authors' understanding of reason as the *final authority*, rejecting the Church, its history and the Bible as sources of God's revelation.[6] Their understanding of reason saw it as *objective* and free from *prejudice* or *tradition* (which they saw as false or flawed). However, reason has a *subjective element* that makes it dependent upon the context or situation in which it has developed and in which it operates.[7] That is, reason was not as objective as they had claimed.

When we try to portray reason as something objective, it then becomes isolated from, and resistant to, any interaction with the truth values of the Bible.[8] Reason, with the use of the spiritual weapons noted by Paul, is not abolished in this process, but brought into subjection to the knowledge of God through Jesus Christ. The movement towards the establishment of a stronghold begins with human reason, perhaps within a demonic conspiracy. It is not reason itself, but its application and use, which begins a process that ends in a stronghold or fortress pitted against God and His purposes and truth.

---

[5] Geoffrey Bromiley, *Theological Dictionary of the New Testament* (Grand Rapids, Michigan: William B Eerdmans Publishing Co, 1985), 536.

[6] Robert Saucy, *Scripture: Its Power, Authority and Relevance* (Nashville: Word Publishing, 2001).

[7] Joel Weinsheimer, *Gadamer's Hermeneutics, a Reading of Truth and Method* (New Haven: Yale University Press, 1985), 167, 169.

[8] Hans Gadamer, *Truth and Method* (New York: Crossroad, 1992), 295-296.

Obstacles or lofty things are "lofty notions" that oppose the knowledge of God. This movement to lofty notions suggests that what began as a false use of reason has now progressed to a level of arrogance which sets up a "wall of rivalry". A wall that now competes with, or argues against, God's anointed leadership and their proclamation of the truth of the gospel.[9] Paul notes that what might begin simply as a thought or idea can develop into a persuasion that is impervious to both the input of God and others. We are capable of getting carried away with an idea that takes us away from God and what He had intended. He also notes that the negativity that flows from this process is quite aggressive in its thought processes and activities. Those whose minds have entered in such strongholds are also active in persuading others to also adopt their philosophy and activities.

One of my friends told the story of his visit as an evangelist to a Pentecostal church in a country district. He had brought with him a young man, who had recently been converted at one of his rallies. Though he knew the pastor of the Church, he did not know the members of the Church. On arrival, he found that the Church deacons had locked the Pastor out of the church because he disagreed with a new spiritual principle they had learnt, whilst the Pastor was away doing a mission. These elders had noted that when the apostles had received the baptism in the Holy Spirit they not only spoke in tongues, but they also had flames of fire upon their heads.

---

[9] Martin, 306. 1991 1991 1991 John Wesley, *Wesley's Notes on the Bible* John Wesley notes that by obstacle or lofty thing Paul refers to "all vain reasonings, and every high thing which exalteth itself as a wall or rampart against the knowledge of God."

The new notion they were teaching was: unless you too experienced flames of fire on your head, as well as speaking in tongues, then you were not properly baptized in the Holy Spirit. The Pastor, of course, spoke against such a novel idea with the result that they had locked him out of the church.

My friend went to the service, they sang some songs and then he rose up to preach. He found the atmosphere so heavy and tense that he just had to sit down again, unable to speak or preach. The young Christian he had brought with him, who knew nothing of what had been going on in the Church, stood up and spoke prophetically from God a message that identified the situation, and how that this new idea had not come from God. The Church deacons at this point repented about what they had been doing, went and got the pastor and brought him back into the Church and apologized. It is so easy to get it wrong and then keep getting it wrong, so that what began as a bad idea, takes on a stronger and stronger hold on our minds so that those thoughts become obstacles and turn into strongholds in our thinking.

The power of such perceptions are immense and dictate both the direction of a person's own life and their attempt to dictate the direction of both the church's life and lives of others. Hersey, Blanchard and Johnson suggest that "People do not behave on the basis of truth and reality. Their behavior is evoked from their perception and interpretation of truth and reality."[10] They are not suggesting that there is no basis for truth and reality, but that people tend to filter out some

---

[10] P Hersey, K Blanchard, and D Johnson, *Management of Organizational Behavior* (Upper Saddle River, NJ: Prentice Hall, 1996), 347-348.

elements of truth and reality. [11] But once the perception has become a "stronghold" then that filtering out process becomes more acute and people tend to develop very selective sight and hearing. Brian Houston writes,

> You should never underestimate the power of what you believe, even if it is only a perception. When you believe something that belief becomes as powerful as if it were the truth.[12]

He notes that negativity affects our perception of truth, because:

> Your outlook depends on what you are looking out from! If you are looking at the world from a heart full of cynicism and bitterness, your perspective of the truth becomes magnified and distorted.[13]

The problem with wrong perceptions is they produce wrong assumptions. And wrong assumptions will produce wrong conclusions, usually because those assumptions are never tested. We also need to be aware that the assumptions we make about other people are often are a result of our own internal perceptions. Jesus said,

> Do not judge so that you will not be judged. For in the way you judge, you will be judged; and by your standard of measure, it will be measured to you. Why do you look at the speck that is in your brother's eye, but do not notice the log that is in your own eye? Or how can you say to your brother, 'Let me take the speck out of your eye'; and behold, the log is in your own eye? You Hypocrite, first remove the log out of

---

[11] Hersey, Blanchard, and Johnson, 347-348.

[12] Houston, 52.

[13] Houston, 52-53.

your own eye, and then you will see clearly to take the speck from your brother's eye.[14]

Imagine someone who has a great big telephone pole sticking out of his eye. Every time he turns around people duck for cover. It is the same with those who have perceptional logs sticking out of their eyes. This perceptional log is like a magnifying lens that magnifies the mistakes and faults of others, whilst minimizing our own. Once we take the perceptional magnifying log out of our own eyes, it is doubtful that we could even find the speck that is in our brother's eye. Jesus calls us to deal with the negative attitudes in our own hearts and lives, so that we can then clearly see the needs of others.

It will also make us more aware of assessing our own assumptions, because we often make decisions based on the assumptions we have made, without ever really finding out the facts. Assumptions are a normal part of the reflection and decision making process. But we look foolish when we act upon untested assumptions, because untested assumptions are rarely right. We need to test our assumptions and prove they are right before we act on them. John Maxwell says, "When we become conditioned to perceived truths and closed to new positive possibilities, the following happens:

- We see what we expect to see, not what we can see;

- We hear what we expect to hear, not what we can hear; and

- We think what we expect to think, not what we can think.[15]

---

14 Matthew 7:1-3 (NASB).

15 John Maxwell, *The Winning Attitude.* 121

Isaiah the Prophet wrote in similar terms:

> Keep on listening, but do not perceive,
> keep on looking, but do not understand,
> render the hearts of this people insensitive,
> their ears dull and their eyes dim,
> lest they see with their eyes, hear with their ears,
> understand with their hearts,
> and return and be healed.[16]

The difficulty with negative thinking is it tends to blow things out of proportion and makes mountains out of molehills. One of the catch phrases we had operating in one of our Churches, was "we were in the business of reducing mountains into molehills." Things really get difficult when they are blown out of proportion, because the repercussions never seem to stop. John Maxwell counters the influence of Murphy's Law which states:

> Nothing is as easy as it looks; everything takes longer than you expect; and if anything can go wrong, it will and at the worst possible moment.[17]

With his own Law, which states:

> Nothing is as hard as it looks; everything is more rewarding than you expect; and if anything can go right, it will and at the best possible moment.[18]

DISCUSSION/REFLECTION QUESTIONS:

1. How does our perception of what we are doing determine the value or meaning of that thing?

---

[16] Isaiah 6:9-10 (NASB).

[17] Maxwell. 121

[18] Maxwell. 122

2. Think of a situation when you had the wrong perception or understanding of what was going on. How did that perception and understanding affect the way you acted? How would you have acted if you had had a more accurate perception and understanding?

3. What can we do in frustrating situations that will enable us to discern God's intentions or purpose in that situation?

4. How do the clichés "bee in her bonnet" or "his mind is set on it" indicate that we may have become entrenched in our thinking?

5. How does the attitude of humility and meekness help us to remain open and flexible in our understanding of the scriptures and what we receive from them?

6. How does loving God with our entire mind assist us in bringing reason into subjection to the knowledge of God through Jesus Christ?

7. Why does Paul instruct us to use spiritual weapons when dealing with people who have allowed their reasoning to become obstacles or "lofty things"?

8. Have you (or some one you know) had an area of your (or his/her) life where you (or he/she) started filtering out elements of truth and reality? Did this area become a "stronghold"? What thoughts or reasoning started this process? How could this process have been changed?

9. Describe instances where people, acting on assumptions, have been entirely wrong. What could they have done so as not to have acted on those assumptions?

10. Describe a situation where a mountain has been made out of a mole hill. What actions could have been done that would have avoided the escalation that occurred?

Chapter Six
Negativity and God's Processes

Negativity works against God's purpose in our lives. Our negative reactions to the situations that confront us in our daily lives prevent us from taking hold of what God wants to do in and through us. However, a positive response to God's work in our lives produces perseverance, character, and hope. Two important passages reflect this process. If God is love, and we are called to be perfect like our Father in heaven is perfect, then God's ultimate goal is that we too become love.[1] John noted this when he wrote,

> Beloved, let us love one another; for love is of God, and he who loves is born of God and knows God... No man has ever seen God; if we love one another, God abides in us and his love is perfected in us... God is love, and he who abides in love abides in God, and God abides in him. In this is love perfected with us, that we may have confidence for the Day of Judgment, because as he is so are we in this world. There is no fear in love, but perfect love casts out fear. For fear has to do with punishment, and he who fears is not perfected in love.[2]

John is convinced that we are called not only to love God but to express that love to others. When we do not love others, then it questions our claim to love God. We are called not only to love others, but to become love to others. It is a matter of establishing love so deeply in our heart and souls that our

---

[1] 1 John 4:7-18; Matthew 5:48.
[2] 1 John 4:7-18 (RSV).

response to others automatically moves to love, because our hearts have become love.

However, in a day and age when the word "love" itself has been abused by both secular and Christian people alike, what type of love are we talking about? The nature of this love is reflected in the process that establishes it in our lives, which ensures that it is not a mushy insipid type of love, but one that is authentic, grounded in scripture and earthed in reality. Peter exhorts his readers in 2 Peter 1:5-7 (NASB) to develop and grow in the following way:

To:	diligence	add	faith
To:	faith	add	moral excellence
To:	moral excellence	add	knowledge
To:	knowledge	add	self-control
To:	self-control	add	perseverance
To:	perseverance	add	godliness
To:	godliness	add	brotherly kindness
To:	brotherly kindness	add	LOVE.[3]

---

[3] E. W. Bullinger, *A Critical Lexicon and Concordance* (London: Samuel Bagster and Sons Limited, 1971), 224. Diligence: comes from the Greek word *spoude* – speed, haste, as manifested in earnestness, diligence, zeal. The word can mean thoroughness; attentiveness; carefulness. p. 27 - The word "add" comes from the Greek word *epichorgeo* – means to furnish or supply beside or further, to superadd. p. 849 - moral excellence: comes from the Greek word *apete*, which means superiority in every respect – in a moral sense, that which gives man his worth, his efficiency, his moral excellence; good quality, excellence of any kind. P. 436 - knowledge in this passage comes from two Greek words: *gnosis and epignosis*, the first referring to knowing, recognition and understanding; the second to clear and exact knowledge, more emphatic because it expresses a more thorough participation on the part of the knower.

Peter writes these words to Christians, not non-Christians. Love is not an automatic response of a redeemed or born-again heart. Love is the result of a process at work in our lives to bring us towards the full stature of the maturity we find in Jesus Christ. Peter tells us that love is the end result of a growth in a number of other characteristics and aspects of our lives. If a Christian is deficient in love then we may need to exhort them to grow in faith, or moral excellence, or knowledge and understanding, or perhaps self-control, or to persevere in the things God has called them to do, or to grow in godliness. Then again we may need to help them grow in brotherly kindness.

It is the contribution of these aspects of our Christian lives that begins to perfect us in LOVE. Peter's exhortation to his readers concludes by saying:

> For if these qualities are yours and are increasing, they render you neither useless nor unfruitful in the true knowledge of our Lord Jesus Christ. For he who lacks these qualities is blind or short sighted, having forgotten his purification from his former sins.[4]

These are not only qualities that we possess, but ones that continue to increase and grow within us. They undergird the effectiveness of our ministry and service to God and others.

Although Paul's outline of this process is more condensed, we will look at it in more detail. In Romans 5:1-5 Paul writes,

> Therefore, having been justified by faith, we have peace with God though our Lord Jesus Christ, [2]through whom also we

---

4 2 Peter 1:8-9 (NASB).

have obtained our introduction by faith into this grace in which we stand; and we exult in hope of the glory of God. [3]And not only this, but we also exult in our tribulations, knowing that tribulation brings about perseverance; [4]and perseverance, proven character, and proven character, hope; [5]and hope does not disappoint, because the love of God has been poured out within our hearts through the Holy Spirit who has been given to us.[5]

The process outlined in verses 3 to 5 form a progression or development of qualities in our lives that release the love of God in our hearts and through us to others. That is:

Tribulation

produces

Perseverance

produces

Proven character

produces

Hope

which is under-girded by

LOVE

This process begins with tribulations, trials and troubles. This is because tribulations or trials are catalysts in our lives for a God inspired growth process. Paul begins the passage by clarifying the underlying foundation of this process, because of our habit to misinterpret the cause and the purpose of tribulations or trials.

---

[5] Romans 5:1(NASB).

In the story of Job, the friends of Job came to counsel him about the catastrophes that had impacted his family and him. Their advice blamed these catastrophes upon hidden sin or arrogance in Job's life. They spent some time trying to discover Job's hidden sins. However, the early chapters of this story tell us that Job was in fact blameless before God and that these catastrophes were a test of Job's faithfulness, not punishment for sin or arrogance. The part of the story I love the most is when God turns up and rebukes Job's friends for their foolish advice and then tells them to ask Job to pray for them. The purpose of the tribulations and trials for Job was for him to discover that no matter how tough things might be, God was still in control. Job needed to learn about the providence of God.[6] Job needed to learn that despite the circumstances that he encountered, disastrous as they may have been, God was still in control of his life.

The Biblical understanding of providence refers to God's lordship over all things. It means to believe that the world was created by God, and continues to be sustained by Him. It goes further than that and entails the sense that God is not only the Lord of history, but also *Lord of our own history*. God not only has a purpose for the world itself, but also a purpose for each one of us.[7] Without a sense of God's providence then Jesus' encouragement for us to ask, seek and knock can make no sense at all.[8] It implies that there is someone there who

---

[6] Book of Job.

[7] Tim Gorringe, *God's Theatre: A Theology of Providence* (London: SCM Press, 1991), 5, 6, 7. Tim challenges what he calls false friends of our understanding of God's providence. They are *interpretations* that have confused a proper understanding of God's providence. These are: fate, chance, fortune, luck, foreknowledge, predestination and determinism.

[8] Matthew 7:7-11

will respond to our asking, seeking and knocking. It also implies that that someone is capable of answering our requests, making known what we seek and is willing to open the door when we knock.

The encounter with tribulations or trials brings us face to face with the movement towards either negativity or cynicism, on the one hand, or positive growth, on the other. It is our response to tribulations and trials that determines which way we will go. It produces negativity and cynicism when we perceive these tribulations as either punishment from God, or God's neglect of our welfare. It produces positive growth when we see these tribulations as opportunities to grow in perseverance, character, and hope. Paul proposes that it is only as we come to the issue of tribulations, trials and trouble in a positive framework that we can truly reflect the love of God that has been poured into our hearts by the Holy Spirit. Paul begins the passage by establishing the foundation upon which these tribulations become a positive force in our lives.

DISCUSSION/REFLECTION QUESTIONS:

1. Do you think God is a positive God? Why?

2. a/ If you answered "yes" to the above question, how much is your response related to the development of perseverance, character and hope?
   b/ If you answer "no" to the above question, how much is your response related to the lack of development of perseverance, character and hope?

3. How much is our understanding of love conditioned by the environment in which we live? Explain.

4. How often do we misinterpret a person's action as a lack of love, when it may well be a lack of some of the other characteristics that Peter outlines in his process that culminates in LOVE? Give an example.

5. Are the qualities that Peter outlines above perfected in us immediately when we become Christians or, rather, are they qualities that grow and develop in our lives over time? Give an example of a quality that has been developed in your life over time. Identify a quality in which you currently need to grow.

6. Do good things come out of tribulations, trials and troubles? Give an example.

7. Do we tend to gravitate more to negativity and cynicism than towards a positive framework that produces prosperity? Why?

8. How important are the foundations of our lives to the things that we try to build on them?

9. Reflect for a moment on the foundations of your life. Do they enable you to grow and develop in the areas of your life that Peter and Paul noted in this chapter?

CHAPTER SEVEN

FOUNDATION FOR POSITIVE GROWTH

> Therefore, having been justified by faith we have peace with
> God though our Lord Jesus Christ. Through whom also we
> have obtained our introduction by faith into this grace in
> which we stand; and we exult in hope of the glory of God [1]

To ensure that we do not get the wrong idea about the
purposes of these tribulations Paul makes it quite clear that
the following process relates specifically to Christians, not
non-Christians. The process of growth that Paul is about to
outline relates to Christians who have a good relationship
with God and are doing what God wants them to do. This
process is not a correction to wayward Christians, or for non-
Christians. It is for the full on man or woman of God who is
doing everything they can to serve and love God. It relates to
people who are already justified before God through faith,
and have peace with God. It is God's means of turning our
hearts into love. Paul's introduction to this process in Romans
5:1-2 carries with it a number of "loaded" Christian terms,
including: "faith", "justified", "peace with God", "grace", "exultation or boasting", "hope", and the "glory of God". Before we
look at the process of growth itself we need to understand the
context of what Paul is saying and the meaning of these key
terms he uses.

FAITH AND JUSTIFICATION

When Paul writes, "therefore, having been justified by faith
we have peace with God though our Lord Jesus Christ" he

---

[1] Romans 5:1-2 (NASB).

emphasizes that we have already been justified before God through our faith. This is something that has already happened, not what needs to happen due to the tribulations or trials that we might be encountering. Faith brings us to a place of justification before God which brings us into a right relationship with God. The result of justification in our lives is that we have peace with God. The word "justified" comes from the Greek word *dikaioo* which originally meant "to put right".[2] As sinners, we have moved away from God, disobeyed His commandments and diverted His purposes to meet our selfish desires. Paul in Ephesians notes that as sinners we are at war with God. He notes that we were dead in our trespasses and sins; sons and daughters of disobedience; following in the Devil's ways; children deserving the wrath of God; strangers to the Kingdom of God; and without hope in the world.[3]

To be justified is to come to a place of reconciliation and peace with God. To justify means "to set forth as righteous, to justify by a judicial act." It refers to something that God does to release us from the guilt of our actions and the punishment for our sins. It is a process by which God frees a person from his or her guilt (which stands in the way of his or her being right with God) and considers him or her to be righteous.[4] Paul wants to make it clear that this process, which leads through trials and tribulation to the development of perseverance, character, and hope, begins when we have

[2] Colin Brown, ed. *The New International Dictionary of New Testament Theology*, 4 vols., vol. 3 (Devon: The Paternoster Press, 1986), 354.

[3] Ephesians 2:1-12.

[4] Bullinger, 429.

already made peace with God, not afterwards. It is a peace and justification that has come about because of our faith in Jesus Christ. Faith is the means by which we come to this peace and it will also be the means by which we will endure the difficulties and troubles that we face in our movement towards growth and prosperity.

FAITH AND GRACE

Faith also connects us to the grace of God. Paul writes: "Therefore, having been justified by faith, we have peace with God though our Lord Jesus Christ, through whom also we have obtained our introduction by faith into this grace in which we stand." God's operating power at work in our lives comes through His "grace". When we are in the thick of troubles and difficulties we cry out for help. We beg him to deliver us from our troubles or tribulation; or send His angels to help us, or better still to send money. However, if the purpose of the troubles and difficulties are aimed at producing love in us, then God does not deliver us from the troubles, nor does He send His angels, nor does He throw in the money. What He sends is more *grace.*

This does not mean that God cannot deliver us, send the angels or more money; nor does it mean that He will not do that. He may in fact deliver us or provide the natural resources we need to solve the problems, difficulties or troubles. However, if God's intention is for us to grow through these difficulties - that is to gain perseverance, character, and hope - then the ingredient we need the most is more grace to persevere. This grace comes to us through the Lord Jesus Christ via the means of our faith. Faith introduces us to the means of grace: the Lord Jesus Christ.

This process of growth is immersed in and surrounded by the grace of God. Paul notes that our faith has brought us into this grace "in which we stand." When the going gets tough, the tough get going. When the going gets tough God pours more grace into our situation than ever before so that we can overcome. Paul uses the Greek word *charis* for grace, which has a number of meanings.[5] The word denotes specifically, God's grace and favor manifested towards people or to an individual, which is a free act of God. As such, it is no more hindered by sin than it is conditional upon works. That means, God does not withdraw His grace from us because of our sin; and God's grace is not given to us because of the good things we might do. It is the grace of God, because it denotes the relationship assumed and maintained by God towards sinful men and women. It is joined with Christ, because it comes to us in and through Him.[6] Jesus died for you when you were still a sinner. Now that you do know God, are submitted to His will, and committed to His purpose, how much more then does God's grace come to you!

The problem we have during tribulation and difficulties is we tend to lose perspective. We sense a lack of the presence of God in the midst of our difficulties and believe He has deserted us when we need Him most. Whilst we bemoan our condition and cry out for God to return; or in some way to indicate that He has not deserted us, God is pouring more of His grace and favor into our situation. As Paul notes:

---

[5] Bullinger, 341. These include: grace, thanksgiving, thanks, favor, pleasure, liberality, gift, benefit, acceptable.

[6] Bromiley, 341.

Law came in, to increase the trespass; but where sin increased, grace abounded all the more, so that, as sin reigned in death, grace also might reign through righteousness to eternal life through Jesus Christ our Lord.[7]

The greater the difficulty or tribulation we may face, the more abundant is the presence of God's grace. When things get harder for us God pumps in more grace to sustain us. It is grace that forms the underlying power, which enables us to stand up and resist the negative forces that have come against us.

God's grace is also aimed at bringing us to a place of reigning in life through Jesus Christ. It is God's means for our overcoming difficulties and prospering in life. To prosper in life means more than simply having an abundance of material possessions. It means a quality of life where we overcome negativity and the debilitating impact of its activity and we sow positively into the lives of others and the needs of the Kingdom of God on earth. The Kingdom of God does not need us to sow into its needs in heaven, but to sow into its needs in the here and now, on earth. Grace brings us to a place of reigning in life in the here and now, as Paul writes:

If, because of one man's trespass, death reigned through that one man, much more will those who receive the abundance of grace and the free gift of righteousness reign in life through the one man Jesus Christ.[8]

Grace moves us from the defeat of sin, and our subsequent condemnation by Law, into God's realm of righteousness, where we can reign in life through Jesus Christ.

---

[7] Romans 5:20-21 (RSV).

[8] Romans 5:17 (RSV).

God's grace brought His Son into the world for us. Jesus came into this world because of our poverty and the power of negativity to defeat us and rob us of the promises and blessings of God. Poverty reaches far beyond the realms of material possessions and riches into the very condition of our soul and spirit. It is the power of sin and the dominion of the devil that has brought our soul and spirit into captivity and shackled us to poverty. Poverty reaches deep into the many relationships we are meant to have with one another, and into our relationship with God. God did a radical thing to deliver us from poverty. Although Jesus Christ was rich, he became poor that we might become rich. Paul writes:

> For you know the grace of our Lord Jesus Christ that though he was rich, yet for your sake he became poor, so that by his poverty you might become rich.[9]

Because we had no power within ourselves to deliver ourselves from the poverty of our soul and spirit, God gave His Son for us that we might truly come alive again in Him. Grace brings us to a frontier of prosperity and riches far beyond the material riches for which our sinful natures crave, a craving that wrongly hopes that the riches themselves will provide meaning and satisfaction in life. When all along it is our being sold out to God and His cause that brings true riches to our soul and prosperity in the things that pertain to meaning and satisfaction in life. That does not mean we do not prosper in material things as well, it is just not conditioned by them.

---

[9] 2 Corinthians 8:9 (RSV).

Although grace is a free gift of God's love for us that we can neither earn nor merit, it comes to us when we come to God in humility, repentance and faith. James writes,

> But he gives more grace; therefore it says, "God opposes the proud, but gives grace to the humble.[10]

Although God's grace is not dependent upon our works or the good things we do, when it comes to the contrast between pride and humility we enter into the realm of a different entity. God takes exception to the sin of pride or arrogance and moves into resist the proud person in his or her endeavours. Pride or arrogance comes from our attempt to own the glory of God independent of God Himself. Pride and arrogance are the strong movement of the human will against the purpose of God and subsequently against His glory. It also results in a heart of defiance against God and what He requires of us as His people. Subsequently then, God does not pour out His grace to those who are proud, but pours out His grace abundantly to those who are humble (this theme is developed further at the end of the next chapter).

DISCUSSION/REFLECTION QUESTIONS:

1. How often do we interpret the troubles and difficulties that we face as God's disfavor, anger or neglect of us in these situations? Why?

2. Why do we need to be made right with God? What means does God use to reconcile us with Himself?

3. How seriously should we take Paul's claim that we have been at war with God? Why?

---

10 James 4:6 (RSV).

4. If our heart is still beating and our brain is still thinking, what does Paul mean when he says we are "dead in our trespasses"?

5. Do you think God really does get angry with us? Why?

6. Why do you think Paul uses legal language when referring to our being justified before God?

7. How tangible do you think "grace" is during times of tribulations, trials and troubles? Explain.

8. During difficult times have you felt a new sense of resolve arise, or a new level of energy emerge for you to overcome those difficulties? How do you think this relates to the essence of grace that Paul describes?

9. Do you think the presence of God's "grace" during times of tribulation, trial or trouble is aimed at transforming the situation we have encountered or transforming us?

10. Why is God so bothered about pride or arrogance?

CHAPTER EIGHT

FOUNDATIONS OF HOPE AND GLORY

> Through whom also we have obtained our introduction by
> faith into this grace in which we stand; and we exult in hope
> of the glory of God.[1]

HOPE

Hope is used twice by Paul in the passage from Romans 5:1-5.
In the first instance, he focuses on the expectation of our
hope: which is the glory of God. In the second instance, he
uses it to relate to one of the stages of our growth that
eventually produces Godly love in us. Paul uses the Greek
word *elpis* for the word hope. It refers to a well-grounded
expectation; or a gladly and firmly held prospect of a future
good. Hope also refers to the expected good for which we
hope.[2] A negative person is a person who has lost hope. They
wallow in the comfort of mediocrity and mundaneness,
because it is easier than holding onto hope in the most trying
of circumstances. But hope is an aspect of our life in God that
helps us to reach beyond the simple possibilities that lie
around us to the impossibilities that lie beyond us. Hope is
one of the three essential qualities of the Christian life,
without which we fail to remain in the centre of God's
purpose and destiny for our lives. Paul writes:

> So faith, hope, love abide, these three; but the greatest of
> these is love.[3]

---

[1] Romans 5:2 (NASB).

[2] Bullinger, 383.

[3] 1 Corinthians 13:13 (RSV).

Central to our possession of hope is having Jesus Christ in our lives, as Paul writes,

> To them God chose to make known how great among the Gentiles are the riches of the glory of this mystery, which is Christ in you, the hope of glory.[4]

Not only is Jesus the centre of our hope, He is also the one who encourages us when we only have just a flicker of hope left. The New Living Translation of Matthew 12:20 notes about Jesus:

> He will not crush those who are weak, or quench the smallest hope, until he brings full justice with his final victory.

Some years ago, when I was studying in theological college, I usually attended the evening chapel service. I had arrived early one evening and knelt to pray and reflect. While I was reflecting, one of the students came in to light the candles. He lit one of the candles and it went out. He tried again and it went out. He then dug into the wax and cleared the wick and lighted it again. It went out. He had another go and finally it stayed alight. As he was doing this Jesus spoke to me and said,

> If the light of God goes out in you I am standing right there beside you to relight the wick.

Paul's first use of hope (*elpis*) in the Romans passage speaks of our long-term walk with God that develops and grows in our possession and experience of the glory of God. Our walk with God goes through ups and downs; highs and lows. Sometimes the "lows" can be so extreme that we feel that God has deserted us, or worse still that we have deserted God. Yet

---

[4] Colossians 1:27 (RSV).

such is the love of Jesus for us that no matter how we fare, in the hustle and bustle of our lives, He is always there to relight the wick of the flame of God in our hearts. When we fall He is there to pick us up, dust us down, heal and restore us, and to send us back into the fray again in His power and strength. Christians turn to negativity when they avoid the processes of God that enable them to persevere through trials and tribulations to gain perseverance, character, and hope.

Paul's second use of the word hope relates to our ongoing hope in the purposes of God. That is, that God will do what He said He would do, and God will fulfil His purpose in and through us. Hope in this context refers to the expectation of things that have not happened or events that have not yet been realised. Paul says,

> If you already have something, you don't need to hope for it. But if we look forward to something we don't have yet, we must wait patiently and confidently" (Romans 8:24-25 NLT).

Hope refers to things that have not yet happened. Hope empowered by faith, will bring about the very things that we are expecting to occur. The empowerment of hope by faith is proclaimed in the Letter to the Hebrews:

> Now faith is the assurance of things hoped for, the conviction of things not seen. For by it the men of old received divine approval. By faith we understand that the world was created by the word of God, so that what is seen was made out of things which do not appear (Hebrews 11:1ff RSV).

The problem we have with hope and expectation is that we have to persevere until the promise comes through. Some Christians give up too early and never see God turn things around to fulfil His word.

Quotes from Leadership Now:

"History has demonstrated that the most notable winners usually encountered heartbreaking obstacles before they triumphed. They won because they refused to become discouraged by their defeats."

— B.C. Forbes

All the adversity I've had in my life, all my troubles and obstacles, have strengthened me... You may not realize it when it happens, but a kick in the teeth may be the best thing in the world for you.

— Walt Disney

He who does not believe in miracles is not a realist.

— Anton Rupert, Rembrandt Group5

Quotes from Keepinsping.Me

Most of the important things in the world have been accomplished by people who have kept on trying when there seemed to be no hope at all.

– Dale Carnegie

Remember that guy that gave up? Neither does no one else.

– Unknown

People are always blaming circumstances for what they are. I don't believe in circumstances. The people who get ahead in this world are the people who get up and look for the circumstances they want, and if they can't find them, make them.

– George Bernard Shaw

Things don't go wrong and break your heart so you can become bitter and give up. They happen to break you down and build you up so you can be all that you were intended to be.

– Charlie Jones

---

[5] Quotes have come from Leading Thoughts (LeadershipNow)
http://www.leadershipnow.com/perseverancequotes.html

When you get to the end of your rope, tie a knot and hang on.
                                          – Franklin D. Roosevelt

Many of life's failures are people who did not realize how close they were to success when they gave up.
                                          – *Thomas Edison*[6]

GLORY

The glory of God provides the backdrop for Paul's exhortation to us to grow through this process, that we might partake of His glory. He uses the Greek word *doxa*. *Doxa* has a number of meanings and is used in a number of ways.[7] In the context of Paul's use of the word in Romans it relates to the appearance of glory which attracts our gaze. It is the manifestation of glory which results in splendour or brightness. It is not the glory of the person or things itself that this relates to, but the very appearance of glory that shines from them.[8]

Glory is used in a number of important ways in the scriptures. Some are:

- **Revival** – revival occurs because God places His Glory upon His People, as Isaiah writes:

  Arise, shine; for your light has come, and the glory of the LORD has risen upon you. For behold, darkness shall cover the earth, and thick darkness the peoples; but the LORD will arise upon you, and his glory will be seen upon

---

6   http://www.keepinspiring.me/quotes-about-not-giving-up-staying-strong/

7   Bullinger, 323. opinion, notion or seeming. Then from the meaning *"seeming"* comes appearance, form, aspect, looks like something, splendour, brilliance, glory.

8   Bullinger, 323.

you. And nations shall come to your light, and kings to the brightness of your rising.[9]

A number of passages in Isaiah proclaim the gathering of the nations to God through His people Israel. In the midst of great darkness – moral, political and philosophical – God's people become beacons or bright lights in that darkness to show the way to God and His Kingdom. The brilliance of that light is the presence and glory of God resting upon His people. True revival comes not simply as a result of human activity, but through the combination of divine and human activity. All the good works, good methods, good prayers and good intentions under the sun would not suffice, if it were not for the glory of God.

- **We are changed by beholding His glory:**

  And we all, with unveiled face, beholding the glory of the Lord, are being changed into his likeness from one degree of glory to another; for this comes from the Lord who is the Spirit.[10]

Paul notes the transforming presence of God in our lives, which unlike the law, is able to transform our broken and sinful nature into the likeness of Jesus Himself, whereby we take on the nature of His glory. Paul describes this as an ongoing process of going from one level of glory to another. Many Christians in the early stages of their Christian lives enjoy the love and presence of God and the excitement of serving Him in His Church and in the world. However, they often fail to go up to the next level of glory,

---

[9] Isaiah 60:1-3 (RSV).

[10] 2 Corinthians 3:18 (RSV).

because the transition from one level of glory to the next is often painful and difficult. It also requires a significant level of change. Because they fail to move to the next level of glory, they also fail to obtain the joy and excitement of that level of glory. Because they have not made the shift in levels they needed to, their Christian life and experience becomes mundane and lifeless.

- **Christ is the source of our glory:**

  To them God chose to make known how great among the Gentiles are the riches of the glory of this mystery, which is Christ in you, the hope of glory.[11]

Here Paul combines the entities of hope and glory and notes that both of these thrive within us only when Jesus Christ is in our lives. Paul does not mean by this that we simply follow Jesus' example and teaching. It means Christ *is in us*. There is an ontological relationship with God that occurs through the actual presence of Jesus Christ in our lives.[12] There is also noted here an expectation, through hope, of participating in God's glory. This participation in God's glory is a significant theme in Paul's teaching, as well as in other New Testament writers such as Peter. Both Paul and Peter link our participation in the glory of God, as fellow heirs with Jesus, with a participation in Jesus' sufferings - sufferings that are not related to

---

[11] Colossians 1:27 (RSV).

[12] Ontological refers to "being" and it relates in this context to our participating in the very nature and being of God, as well as being brought into the fellowship or communion that the Father, the Son and the Holy Spirit have with one another. See *Holiness without the Law* by Andrew Peters.

sickness or sin, but in sharing in the proclamation of the kingdom of God and living our lives as men and women of God.[13]

Glory is one of the fundamental aspects of life that we desire, but one that we feel uneasy about owning. The reason for this is that sin has robbed us of the real glory of God. It has been substituted with a false, human centred, inadequate source of honour or esteem. The origins of sin began with a desire for God's glory *independent* of God Himself. The attempt to claim glory independent of God was first Lucifer's, and then Adam and Eve's fundamental mistake. For Lucifer, it brought about his fall from heaven and eventual exclusion from both the heavenly and earthly realms. For Adam and Eve, and subsequently for the whole human race, it resulted in exclusion from the Garden of Eden and the Tree of life (eternal life) and resulted in spiritual, relational and physical death.

The attitudes of pride and arrogance lie at the heart of the desire for God's glory independent of God Himself.[14] In answer to the impact that sin in our lives, with its roots in

---

[13] Romans 8:15f (RSV) – "For you did not receive the spirit of slavery to fall back into fear, but you have received the spirit of sonship. When we cry, "Abba! Father!" It is the Spirit himself bearing witness with our spirit that we are children of God, and if children, then heirs, heirs of God and fellow heirs with Christ, provided we suffer with him in order that we may also be glorified with him."

[14] Andrew Peters, *Heirs of the Kingdom*, seminar notes. (Genesis 1-2; Isaiah 14:12ff; Ezekiel 28:11ff) Isaiah notes Lucifer's desire for God's throne and glory with the five I wills: I will ascend into heaven; I will exalt my throne above the stars of God; I will sit also upon the mount of the congregation, in the sides of the north; I will ascend above the heights of the clouds; and I will be like the most High (Isaiah 14:12ff).

pride and arrogance, God not only calls us to repent and follow Jesus Christ, but also to develop a *spirit of humility* (James 4:5-7). In the passages on humility found in James, Peter and Proverbs[15] the "humble" have been consistently contrasted with the "proud." Pride was a central element in Satan's original sin. He wanted to live life on his own terms rather than submit to the LORD God as the creature he was. We also followed in his ways and have wanted to live our lives on our own terms, rather than to submit to the will of God. The movement towards humility also brings a new and different search for wisdom, a wisdom that comes from God and not us. That process rejects the false notion that we can acquire wisdom by human powers alone.[16] It is only as we turn back to a true dependence on God and His purpose and will for our lives that we gain access to the glory of God.

DISCUSSION/REFLECTION QUESTIONS:

1. What signs does a negative person give that he or she has lost hope?

2. How does a loss of hope bring about a sense of mediocrity or mundaneness?

3. What is it about the nature and being of Jesus that makes Him the hope of glory?

4. Does hope relate to things we already have or things that we do not yet have? Give an example.

5. How does the appearance of God's glory upon His church lead to people becoming Christians?

---

[15] James 4:5f; 1 Peter 5:4f; Proverbs 3:34; Luke 18:9.f.

[16] T. Desmond Alexander and Brian Rosner, "New Dictionary of Biblical Theology," (2001).

6. How do the things we focus upon, whether negative or positive, affect what we become in the future? How does this relate to what Paul says about Jesus in 2 Corinthians 3?

7. Why has sin and pride robbed us of the true glory of God?

8. Why is humility a powerful force in our lives and activities?

CHAPTER NINE
DEVELOPMENT OF PERSEVERANCE

And not only this, but we also exult in our tribulations, knowing that tribulation brings about perseverance; and perseverance, proven character, and proven character, hope; and hope does not disappoint, because the love of God has been poured out within our hearts through the Holy Spirit who has been given to us.[1]

EXULTING IN TRIBULATIONS

Tribulations, difficulties and troubles are a sign of God's growth process at work in our lives. Our problem with difficulties and troubles is that we interpret them to be the negative things going on in our life, when they are the stepping stones to a victorious and prosperous life. We also interpret these situations to be the result of God's disfavour, or anger at us for something we have done. As we noted earlier, tribulations, difficulties and troubles are not God's disfavour or His anger at us, but God's process to develop and grow us so that we can reach our full potential, that we can grow to the full stature of Jesus Christ. Paul uses the Greek word *thlipsis* to refer to these tribulations, difficulties and troubles. Thlipsis has a variety of meanings which include "burden", "anguish", "affliction", "tribulation", "persecution", and "trouble".

There are three ways this term is used in the Old and New Testament: 1/ it refers to justified affliction and trouble that are a result of us leaving God and His ways; 2/ it refers to

---

[1] Romans 5:3-5 (NASB).

unjustified affliction and trouble that have come because we belong to God, are committed to His purpose and aim to live in righteousness; and 3/ it refers to the transforming process of God in our lives to strengthen our character and develop our personality. Our use of the term in this study revolves predominately around the third way, but also includes the second. For a more detailed outline of these three ways see APPENDIX 2.

The various uses of this term indicate that these tribulations, difficulties and troubles bring with them great pressure and stress.[2] We can become extremely distressed under the affliction they bring.[3] One sense of the use of this word means to press, squash or hem you in. When you encounter activity noted under the term *thlipsis* you can be sure that you will feel quite uncomfortable, being both harassed and vexed. Philosophically, this group of words is used for life's afflictions.[4] In contemporary language, it can mean to find yourself "between a rock and a hard place."

---

[2] Bullinger, 30,820. *thlipsis* can mean "Pressure, compression, straightness; hence pressure from evils, affliction, distress".

[3] Brown, ed., 807.

- The noun *thlipsis*, which means oppression, distress, affliction, is linked with the verb *thlibo.*
- It is occasionally found coupled with *stenochoria* (derived from *stenos* and *steinos*, meaning narrow, and *choria*, meaning space, place), which from Thucydides onwards is used to express a narrow place, and hence being pressed by inner and outer difficulties.
- Literally *Thlibo* means: "to press," "squash," "hem in," then "to be narrow".
- Literally *Thlipis* means, "pressure" in the physical sense, to put pressure on.
- Figuratively *Thlibo* means "to afflict," 'harass" with the nuances a) "to discomfort"; b) "to oppress" or "vex".

[4] Bromiley, 334.

When these tribulations, difficulties and troubles arrive you can guarantee the going gets tough. As they say, "when the going gets tough then the tough get going". Our issue is: just where do the tough get going to. Remember tribulation, difficulties and troubles can easily lead us into negativity and cynicism, when God intended them to work in us a positive, life-enhancing, life-giving process called perseverance, character, and hope. Too many people have turned to hardness and bitterness as their defensive reaction to the disappointments that life tends to bring. So what does Paul say we should do when life's afflictions come our way?

Paul tells us to "exult" or "boast" in our tribulations. Our Australian language has incredible nuances when it comes to dealing with tough times. Statements like "Great!" or "Thanks!" are used in such a way to express to God or others, a sense of "don't do me any more favours!" In other words we use these statements in quite negative ways to try to take the bite out of the trouble, difficulties and troubles that have come our way. When Paul tells us to exult or boast in our tribulations he calls us instead to use such statements in quite a positive way. Rather than resenting the arrival of another trouble or difficulty we should in fact welcome them as an opportunity to grow and develop in perseverance, character, and hope.

In this passage from Romans Paul uses two Greek words that can be translated "glory". The first one is *doxa* noted above. The second one, *kauchaomai*, means "to speak loud", "be loud-tongued", "boast" or "vaunt one's self".[5] Paul uses *kauchaomai*, twice in this passage. The first time, he uses it in

---

[5] Bullinger, 324.

the introduction to encourage us to boast in our hope of attaining the glory of God, which we noted earlier. The second, is to "boast" or "exult" in our tribulations. This has the sense of being quite prolific in our boasting. This is a significant statement from Paul, who since the Damascus road event was totally against boasting altogether.[6] However, here he uses it in a similar sense as James' exhortation for us to rejoice in our sufferings and trials,[7] and Jesus' exhortation for us to rejoice in our persecutions.[8] The purpose of such boasting is to take the real bite out of the tribulations, difficulties, troubles or afflictions that have come upon us. It also re-orientates us in such a way that we can deal with such tribulations and troubles in a positive rather than a negative manner.

Be sure that Paul does not intend us to accept these tribulations, difficulties and troubles as our "lot" in life; nor does he intend that we wear them as a burden we have to endure or a cross we have to carry. That is not Paul's intention. His intention is that we overcome these tribulations, difficulties and troubles – that is, we come through them. He also intends for us, in the process, to grow in perseverance, character, and hope. Negativity drives us to flee from such tribulations, difficulties and troubles; and to avoid

---

[6] Paul recognised his own arrogance and boasting when he zealously sought to destroy the Christian sect and all its adherents. His encounter with Jesus on the Damascus road challenged him to the depth of his being and showed how wrong he could be in boasting that he was the one who knew God and His purposes. It is not unusual then to find Paul consistently exhorting us to turn away from boasting in anything but Jesus Himself – "so that no man may boast before God... so that, just as it is written, "LET HIM WHO BOASTS, BOAST IN THE LORD." (1 Corinthians 1:29,31).

[7] James 1:2-4.

[8] Matthew 5:10-12.

dealing with them and overcoming them. It also means that we fail to grow. Exulting and boasting in our tribulations also assists us in the first stage of this growth – to grow in perseverance, patience and endurance.

PERSEVERANCE

The first stage of growth through tribulation, difficulties and troubles is to grow in our ability to hang in there, no matter what the odds and how difficult the situation. Paul uses the Greek word *hypomone* to refer to perseverance, patience and endurance. The word has the sense of "a bearing-up under" the pressure, affliction and discomfort that tribulations, difficulties and troubles bring. Thus the word means "patience or endurance, a holding out until the tribulation is past, the difficulty is overcome or the trouble recedes".[9] The verb *hypomeno*, found since the time of Homer, and subsequently Plato meant "to remain behind" or "stand one's ground." It meant that instead of fleeing from the trouble at hand we stand and face it head on, to overcome rather than succumb to the forces at work in the tribulation, difficulty or trouble. It meant to survive the ordeal we are going through, and to "remain steadfast" or "persevere" through the time of trouble.[10] Such perseverance, patience and endurance are essential to: being successful as Christians; producing fruit for the kingdom of God; and completing the race that is set before us. The importance of such perseverance is noted by both Jesus and the writer of the Letter to the Hebrews:

---

[9] Bullinger, 574.
[10] Brown, ed., 772.

And as for that in the good soil, they are those who, hearing the word, hold it fast in an honest and good heart, and bring forth fruit with patience.[11]

Therefore, since we are surrounded by so great a cloud of witnesses, let us also lay aside every weight, and sin which clings so closely, and let us run with perseverance the race that is set before us, looking to Jesus the pioneer and perfecter of our faith, who for the joy that was set before him endured the cross, despising the shame, and is seated at the right hand of the throne of God.[12]

Such perseverance does not mean letting people walk all over you, or continuing in poor and abusing relationships, but to stand your ground in the things that God has called you to do. Patience is not a matter of putting up with bad behaviour from others, but being all that God wants you to be.

It is important to note that there are some difficulties and troubles that we really need to walk away from, because they are totally destructive and hopeless. However, it is often difficult to judge when we should do so. Winkie Pratney notes *that it is not over until Jesus says it is over.* Winkie tells the following story:

God called a young minister and his wife into Harlem in 1970s, during the time when the *Black Panthers* were the dominant gang. There was a rival gang called the *Low Riders* because they took the springs out of their cars that made them ride very low to the road. The Black Panthers took issue with this ministry couple because of the positive influence they were having with some of the young African-American children. They began ringing and threatening them, telling them to leave. The couple prayed each time a

---

[11] Luke 8:15 (RSV).

[12] Hebrews 12:1 (RSV).

threat came and hung in there because God had not told them to leave. Finally, the Black Panthers rang to say they were on their way to kill them. The couple prayed and asked God to send angels to protect them. The Black Panthers never got to their house because the Low Riders, had heard about the threat. Because they liked this couple they surrounded the block, on which their home was located, with their cars and stood on the top of their cars with baseball bats and other weapons. When the Black Panthers arrived and saw the Low Riders, they turned away because they did not want to get into a brawl with the Low Riders.[13]

When the going gets really tough, God can send us some very unusual people to assist us in the work He has called us to do. However, there are times when God calls us to walk away from some really difficult situations. If He says it is over then it is really over.

DISCUSSION/REFLECTION QUESTIONS:

1. Why does God think that tribulations, difficulties and troubles have the potential to bring out the best in us?

2. Is there a connection between finding ourselves "between a rock and a hard place" and a sense of achievement and satisfaction?

3. What type of things can we say or do that would be exulting or boasting in our tribulations, difficulties and troubles?

4. Is there a trial or difficulty you (or someone you know) are going through at the moment? How could you (or he or she) boast, exult or rejoice in that situation?

---

[13] Taken from one of Winkie Pratney's messages about ministry to the counter-culture.

5. What types of situations tempt us to become negative or downhearted?

6. To what extent could perseverance be seen as building up our spiritual muscles?

7. Why is patience not letting people treat you as a doormat and walk all over you; or putting up with rude and inconsiderate behaviour?

8. In regards to perseverance how helpful is the statement, "it is not hard, it just takes work"? Why?

9. What fruit do you think comes from perseverance? Be specific.

CHAPTER TEN
DEVELOPMENT OF CHARACTER

The development of perseverance, patience and endurance sets us up to take on the next stage in our process of growing in perseverance, character, and hope; that is our growth in "character" or "proven character". Our character basically reflects who we are in our innermost being; what we really stand for; and how we treat those who are close to us in personal relationships and loyal to us in leadership relationships. Paul uses the Greek word *dokime*, which means to prove or test a person's ability to be steadfast in difficult situations and testing times.[1] It is through such testing processes that their true worth, reliability and genuineness can be seen.[2] A person who has proven character is one who, through the trials and difficulties has been found to be reliable and genuine – and as a result, recognized, trusted and esteemed.[3] When a person avoids the testing ground of perseverance, through various tribulations, difficulties and troubles, then the failure to develop certain aspects of character is also recognised and subsequently he or she is found to be wanting.

---

[1] Bullinger, 259. Bullinger notes that the Greek word means "proof", "trial"; either "the state of being tried" or "the state of having been tried", "tried", "probity", "approved integrity".

[2] Bromiley. Bromiley notes that the root word *dokimos* means "tested," and thus to be found a) "reliable," and b) "esteemed," or "valuable." *Dokimion* has the sense of "tested," "genuine".

[3] Brown, ed., 808. Brown notes that *dokimos* means – "trustworthy", "reliable", "tested", "recognized", "used as a technical term for genuine", "current coinage", "but also applied to persons enjoying general esteem". Also that *Dokime* – "approved character".

None of us enjoy being tested and tried. However, the good side of perseverance is it testifies to our proven character. When I began preaching back in 1974, I felt that I could not preach unless I also did some biblical and theological study as well. I wanted to be sure that I was preaching the right things. I therefore submitted myself to a life-long process of allowing qualified scholars, pastors and teachers to examine my theology. These people came from very diverse theological and biblical backgrounds.

Let me tell you, it was not always pleasant, especially when my own theological position was quite different from those who were teaching me, and worse, those who were examining my work, and fundamentally my theology. Despite the diversity of these examiners and testers, I usually did pretty well, gaining credits, distinctions and an occasional high distinction, except for one subject where I only received a pass. I remember challenging the lecturer on a mark for an essay where I only received 53%. I told him he was biased on the topic that I had written on. He gave it to his co-lecturer to check and he also gave me 53%. But he was just as biased as the other one, in my thinking. Reading the essay again myself, some years later, yes the lecturer was biased, but the essay was only worth 53%.

When I look back over those years, I still basically hold my original theological and biblical position, much more refined than when I began, of course. The value of the testing was the building up of a confidence in the theological and biblical understanding I have; and its application to the pastoral, evangelistic, teaching and ministry development work that I do. I value the testing and examining processes that I have been through; because each of them required that I develop and grow in certain aspects of my life. I had to grow in character. There were times when I stumbled, but I had to fight my way through and persevere in the midst of the testing.

I remember having worked on a paper on Arianism one evening.[4] I was so disgusted with my efforts that I threw the completed essay in the waste paper basket. Whilst later having coffee with a friend, she asked how the essay was going. I told her in no uncertain terms where it had landed. She dug it out of the waste paper basket, read it and told me it was really good. I didn't believe her, but at her encourage-ment submitted it for marking. I received a high distinction mark of 90% for it, with the comment from the examiner, "I do not mind reading material over the word limit that it as good as this!" I learnt that day that we are not always good assessors of the work we do. However, in my college days not everyone survived the testing. I know fellow students who had studied with me in those early days, who resented and

---

4 Sinclair B. Ferguson and David F Wright, *New Dictionary of Theology* (Downers, Grove, IL: InterVarsity Press, 2000, c1988), 42.; G.T. Kurian, *Nelson's New Christian Dictionary* (Nashville: Thomas Nelson Publishers, 2001), Arianism. Arianism was a false or heretical theological position began by Arius (250-336 A.D.) who was a presbyter in Alexandria. Arianism denied the full divinity of Christ. Arius held that the Son of God was not eternal but was created before the foundation of the world by the Father. He was therefore not God by nature, but a creature. His dignity as Son of God was bestowed on him as a gift. Full divinity and the worship that goes with it belongs uniquely to the Father. The council of Nicaea that met to debate this issue define the faith of the Christian church as believing in the coeternity and coequality of the three persons of the Trinity. That is, Jesus, as the Son of God, is divine – He is God, with the Father and the Holy Spirit.

resisted the testing process. They have not prospered in ministry and life, standing as burnt out wrecks along life's highway. They did not persevere and develop proven character, and it shows.

Character is often referred to as moral fibre. The reason for this is that character is the result of standing our ground in the most difficult situations. It is a matter of hanging in when everything tells us to split. It results in a continuing on when everything is telling you to turn back. It is a matter of staying the course until God calls it quits. Those who produce character find that God always comes through. He may seem to be late or tardy to us, but He never arrives before it is too late. They also discover that the most unusual results come from the waiting process related to perseverance and patience. They often see the other side of the trial or tribulation because they did not give up in the midst of it. They discover hope in the most hopeless of situations, because they have been tested in the fire and have overcome.

The Book of Daniel gives two examples of character producing a God orientated miracle. The first was Daniel and his friends' refusal to eat the Babylonian king's choice food, because of the observance of their own religious food laws. Their overseer was concerned at reprisals if they were to deteriorate in health because of a lack of eating the king's choice food. They made an agreement with the overseer that if within ten days their health was deteriorating then they would eat the king's choice food. Ten days later they were much healthier than all the others who had succumbed to the king's luxurious life.[5]

---

[5] Daniel 1:8-16.

The second was the case of Shadrach, Meshach and Abed-nego who refused to bow down and worship the statue of the Babylonian king Nebuchadnezzar.[6] As a result they were thrown into a fiery furnace to die because they would not bow to the king. The two soldiers who threw them into the fire instantly died because of the intensity of the heat. However, there in the midst of the fire they met with a fourth person who may have been an angel or God Himself. They were neither harmed by the fire, singed, nor were their clothes burnt. Upon calling them out of the fire, the king bowed to their God Yahweh.

DISCUSSION/REFLECTION QUESTIONS:

1. Why is character more important than good looks or even talent in a person's life?

2. Why does character develop via perseverance during difficult and trying times, rather than during good times?

3. Is genuineness in a person's life and relations important? Why?

4. Do you find unreliable people hard to work with? Why?

5. What effect does a lack of character have upon the purpose of our lives? Why?

6. What results have you seen in your own life or in the lives of people you know because you or they have persevered in a difficult and trying situation?

---

6 Daniel 3:19-30

7. Is there an area in your life where you have not persevered
    or had patience, in which you need to address anew and
    grow in that area?

CHAPTER ELEVEN

DEVELOPMENT OF HOPE AND LOVE

And hope does not disappoint, because the love of God has been poured out within our hearts through the Holy Spirit who has been given to us.[1]

HOPE

We looked earlier at hope in the context of its long-term expectation of our sharing in the glory of God. The understanding of the term hope, now used by Paul in this process of growth, takes on a different quality and meaning. It refers to a hope that is not disappointed - a hope that overcomes the obstacles that stand before it. Hope used in this context is the hope of someone who has: been through the fire; persevered through the tribulations and trials; stood in his or her integrity; and found that God turned up in the nick of time and turned the situation around. Hope springs up in the heart of those who have been tested and have found that the impossible gives way to those who stand steadfast in what God has called them to do.

Hope is the motivator that enables us to break through the temptations to despair and cynicism. Hope is what keeps us focused upon God's agenda rather than the negative impact of the forces at work in the situations we face. Hope enables us to be established in the purpose of God and stand centred in that purpose. For Paul, "this hope does not disappoint us" completes the climax of this process of God in our life, which takes us from the despair of negativity to overcoming and

---

[1] Romans 5:3-5 (NASB).

prosperity. "The hope which is thus strengthened and confirmed does not put those who cherish it to shame by proving illusory".[2] God does not forsake, nor let down, those who stand in His name, persevere in times of difficulty and grow in proven character.

Some years ago God gave me a vision of a forest that had been devastated by fire. Everything was burnt, black and demolished. In the midst of this blackened landscape there were stick like figures bent over and black like everything else. As I watched they stood up straight in the midst of the devastation around them. The Lord said that a fire had gone through His Church that had not come from Him. The stick figures I saw were men and women who had gone through the fire and had survived. They had been burnt by the fire of cynicism and pessimism that had ravaged the Church. The Lord said that these men and women of God, who had stood through the fire, were going to rise up and lead the Church in the things of God.

Cynicism means to be sceptical of goodness and to sneer at those who attempt to live in righteousness and integrity. It interprets goodness and righteousness as naivety. Cynicism aims to tear off the veil from human weakness and to strip leaders of their authority by the use of innuendos and murmuring. Pessimism on the other hand believes that the evil of life outweighs the good. It is the tendency to expect the worst outcome and has a disposition to take the gloomiest possible view. It produces defeatism, despair, hopelessness, and despondency. The effect of cynicism and pessimism is to

---

[2] C.E.B Cranfield, *A Critical and Exegetical Commentary on the Epistle to the Romans* (Edinburgh: T & TClark Ltd, 1975), 251-252.

produce in the person an underlying impervious sheath that prevents growth in maturity and negates the purifying work of God's refining fire. This underlying impervious sheath produces in a person a defensive behavior which makes him or her resistant to instruction and learning by the development of an unteachable spirit. It produces unbelief and a sense of hopelessness, which produces murmuring and grumbling and a negative picture of life. This results in disloyalty, and a mistrust that doubts other people's motives.

Those who exhibit hope in the same situations and circumstances, which have produced in others cynicism and pessimism, have learnt the power of God resident in perseverance during times of trouble and have developed a proven character. They are those who have tapped into the hidden resources of God and the abundant life Jesus has given to us. Hope is about expectation; those who hope expect that God will turn up just in time to meet whatever the need might be. Hope brings to the forefront of our hearts and minds a faith that produces obedience to God and His purposes.

Whereas cynicism and pessimism, on the one hand, produce a sense of hopelessness and deep resentment, on the other hand, those who hope in difficult circumstances often find resources available to them that others never seem to find. Jesus said, "For whoever has, to him more will be given, and he will have abundance; but whoever does not have, even what he has will be taken away from him."[3] Those who have are those who have learnt to use the resources they already have available to them, rather than being anxious about what

---

[3] Matthew 13:12. (NKJV).

they do not have. By using their current resources to the full they find that as they do that those resources begin to multiply. They have learnt that the pursuit of excellence in all that we do is not the achievement of perfection, but doing the best you possibly can with the resources you have available. Too often we focus on what we do not have and fail to utilize what God has already given to us. For example:

> On one occasion we had been visited by the wardens (or elders) of a nearby church to see what we did in worship and ministry. One of the wardens commented that we were so fortunate to have so any musicians in our church, where they had none. I responded by telling them that they probably did have some musicians in their congregation, but had not yet discovered their presence. They denied this possibility strenuously for some time until one of them noted that in fact they had a concert pianist in their congregation. As they noted this I immediately had a vision of a strategically placed grand piano in their church played by this concert pianist.

I have found that even in the poorest of churches or groups that there are unused resources sitting there, either not recognized or utilized by the church and its leaders. By using what God has already given to us we begin to tap the fountain of additional resources we might need. The greatest of these resident resources we have is the love of God which has been poured into our hearts by the Holy Spirit and needs to be released in our lives and poured out to others.

LOVE:

We now move to the issue of love. Paul does not present love as the next and last step in the long process that has gone from sufferings to perseverance to proven character to hope. The presence of the love of God in our lives in fact precedes this process that leads from sufferings to hope. This love has been poured into our hearts by the Holy Spirit, who has been given to us. That the Holy Spirit has already been given to us indicates that just like faith, love is something we have resident in our hearts before this process begins. The process does not occur so that we can obtain the love of God in our lives. It has already been poured out into our hearts. Paul's use of the metaphor "poured out" carries with it a sense that the love of God has been lavished upon us, abundantly given through the coming of the Holy Spirit into our lives.[4] No Christian has a short supply of God's love in their lives, even though there are times when they do not use it.

Paul substantiates this claim, not so much by the subjective reception of the Holy Spirit in our lives, but by the act of God giving His Son for us whilst we were still sinners, whilst we were still enemies of God. Paul writes, "While we were still weak, at the right time Christ died for the ungodly…But God shows his love for us in that while were yet sinners Christ died for us."[5] God's love was poured out for us over 2,000 years ago when Jesus went to the cross for us. It was a love given to us undeserved; and it always remains a love given to us, undeserved. We can do nothing that merits or earns God's love for us. It is the nature of this love that leads Paul to the conclusion that it not only undergirds this hope, but also guarantees that the expectations of this hope will be realized.

The reason that this hope, which has been born in the fire of problems and difficulties, does not disappoint us is because it is undergirded by God's love. Hope that emerges from proven

---

[4] Cranfield, 253.

[5] Romans 5:6,8 (RSV).

character produces an integrity that will always bear the fruit of its expectations. There is a difference between hope that has come forth out of the process that Paul describes and the illusion and fantasies that arise in those who avoid this process. The type of hope that does not bear the fruit of its expectation, or that which disappoints us, has not persevered during the time of trouble and difficulty and therefore does not contain the element of proven character. Without persever-ance and proven character hope becomes illusory, and is often not fulfilled because the holder of the hope doesn't last the distance between the birth of the hope and its fulfilment.

Those who do not persevere through the difficulties and troubles and produce proven character either: 1/ do not put in the needed work and effort for the hope to come to realization; or 2/ press the self-destruct button just before the hope reaches its pinnacle of fulfilment. For many people the threat and fear of success is greater than the hoped-for benefits of that success. Because they have not overcome through perseverance and proven character then success becomes a threat rather than a reward for the hard work they have done to gain that success.

Christians who move into negativity often have a subtle feeling or belief that either God no longer loves them or they no longer deserve that love. Paul goes on to make the point that:

> Since, therefore, we are now justified by his blood, much more shall we be saved by him from the wrath of God. For if while we were enemies we were reconciled to God by the death of his Son, much more, now that we are reconciled,

shall we be saved by his life. Not only so, but we also rejoice in God through our Lord Jesus Christ, through whom we have now received our reconciliation.[6]

There arises subtly in the minds of Christians who move into negativity, cynicism and despair that somehow or other they have offended God and He no longer cares for them. Paul's point is that God gave His Son for us when we were yet sinners, when we were enemies of God and living under His wrath; how much more does that love of God apply to those who have responded to that love and turned to follow God in their lives through Jesus Christ. It is important that we note that God's love is not earned nor merited by anything we do. It is always a result of His grace and love for us, both before and after we become Christians. The guarantee of this is the gift of the Spirit who is not only the proof but also the means by which God's love is poured into our hearts.[7]

DISCUSSION/REFLECTION QUESTIONS:

1. Is the "impossible dream" simply an illusion of a hopeful mind, or the focus upon unseen resources that come into being through faith (see Hebrews 11:1ff)?

2. Why do we seem more readily to fall into despair and cynicism than to hold onto the hope that is set before us?

3. Why is it important to maintain an open and teachable soul and spirit within us?

---

6 Romans 5:9-11.

7 Raymond Brown, Joseph Fitzmeyer, and Roland Murphy, *The New Jerome Biblical Commentary* (New Jersey: Geoffrey Chapman, 1990), 844.

4. Are mumbling and grumbling always indications of a cynical and pessimistic heart?

5. Why do you think God responds to an expectant heart and mind?

6. Why don't we deserve God's love?

7. If we do not deserve God's love why do you think He loved us anyway?

8. How does love relate to hope and the fulfilment of what hope promises?

9. How does love help us overcome the fear of success (see 1 John 4:15-19)?

10. In reference to Romans 5:9-11, quoted above; does God's love apply to us more now that we have turned away from being His enemies to being His friends?

APPENDIX ONE: CYNICISM & PESSIMISM

[IONA CHRONICLES VOL. 4 NO 1 - 2010: LEADERSHIP DYNAMICS PART ONE used with permission]

INTRODUCTION

Some years ago the Lord gave me a vision of a burnt out forest where all the trees had been completely demolished by a fierce fire. There were only thin sticks still standing. Suddenly these sticks began to move and they represented men and women who had gone through the fire and were completely covered in ash. The Lord told me that a *fire* had ravaged His church that had not come from Him. The figures I saw moving were men and women of God who had gone through the fire and survived, blacken though they might be. These men and women were going to rise up and lead His Church into the future. The fire that had ravaged His Church was *cynicism*.

Sometime before this vision we had been through such a ravaging fire in one of our churches. A group of lay leaders in the church initially began highlighting my weaknesses and criticised my leadership because of those weaknesses. However, when that did not seem to daunt me they began on my strengths; attributing impure motives to all that I did. I felt stripped raw from the ongoing criticism and murmuring. During that period I remember attending an evening service at an Assemblies of God church we visited. I had asked God to give me a word as I was feeling pretty low. During the service the visiting evangelist was preaching a gentle message on God's healing power. In the middle of the message he stopped and did a complete detour from the message he was preaching.

He asked the congregation what was the name of the man in the Old Testament who had three sons; and the names of his sons. We informed him that he was talking about Noah and his sons Ham, Shem and Japheth.[1] He then compared the difference between the actions of Ham who exposed his father's nakedness and his two brothers who covered up that nakedness. He told us that not only should we support our leaders in their strengths, but to also cover up their weaknesses (these weaknesses do not refer to immorality). To expose our leader's weaknesses was similar to Ham's action of exposing his fathers' nakedness. I felt God lifting my spirit up as he spoke those words, even though they totally messed up the flow of his message on healing. Upholding a leader's strengths and covering up his or her weaknesses is totally opposite to the ravaging effect of cynicism upon the church's life and leadership. Cynicism often arises in people's hearts when they suffer from leadership malnutrition. The effect of such malnutrition is to ill-equip a leader or team member for the difficulties that ministry or leadership brings and the failures that often occur. This can lead to the development of cynicism and pessimism in a leader or team member's life and ministry.

LEADERSHIP MALNUTRITION:

Leadership malnutrition occurs when a person has not had enough training for the work that he or she is expected to do.

---

[1] Genesis 9: 19-23.

It is not that there is no training, but it is not enough to equip them for the difficulties they will face in ministry in the church and the world. This includes training our leaders in the wrong dynamics for the work we expect them to do. In addition to the lack of training there also occurs a lack of support for them as they attempt to do that ministry. There is no real process to discern their actual skills, gifts and abilities and they are often appointed to areas of ministry and leadership that they are not equipped or gifted to do. Or they are appointed too early to leadership positions that they are not mature enough to handle. Paul notes that we should not appoint a new Christian to a leadership position too early lest they be lifted up in pride and fall into the trap by the devil.[2] As leaders we are often pressured by circumstances to promote people far too early in their development of maturity and neither they or us survive the outcomes. Yet if we wait and develop them then they bear fruit for their efforts.

In one church we had in country Victoria, I had felt in prayer that one of our young men should be our children's ministry leader. The problem was that he and his wife were not happy with our new contemporary music and disagreed with what we trying to do with the children's ministry. There was no way that I could appoint him to that position whilst he had trouble with our music and children's ministry. We decided to love and nurture them until God showed us they were ready. Sometime later, at a Parish Council (Church Board) meeting, which consisted of representatives from our six churches, an older man from one of our traditional churches commented

---

[2] 1 Timothy 3: 6.

that they didn't like the new music we had at our main contemporary church. As this just came from left field, without any instigation, there was complete silence in the room. Then this voice rang out from beside me and noted "We don't like the music you have at your church either." I turned to see who had spoken, and was surprised to discover that it was the young man who had previously disagreed with our contemporary music. Now he was defending it. Something had changed. He not only liked our music, but when I spoke to him at his home later, he really began to see what we were trying to do with our children's ministry. Under his leadership the new family and children's ministry called the *Simpson Street Family* became one of the best areas of ministry we had in our church.

Malnutrition in leaders also arises because they have had little or no debriefing during difficult times and they find no place to share the problems and difficulties they incur. Such leaders are also given no real direction for their area of leadership or ministry and do not receive clear definition of the boundaries of their ministry and leadership. This occurs when the leader, who delegated them to their position, abandons them; makes no time for them; and secures no ongoing direct links with them.[3] This, coupled with an ongoing lack of appreciation and encouragement, means that when they meet with obstacles and problems in achieving any real growth in their area of ministry they have nowhere to go to resolve those problems. It is from such processes or

---

[3] Hersey, Blanchard, and Johnson, 206. They note the following ineffective leadership dynamics have a negative effect on developing new leaders: abandoning, dumping, avoiding and withdrawing.

lack of processes that the seeds of cynicism and pessimism are sown in the hearts of budding leaders.

LEADERSHIP CONDITION

Cynicism is an attitude which is sceptical of, and sneers at, goodness – it interprets it as naivety. Cynicism is given to tearing off the veil from human weakness – finding the weaknesses of leaders and attempting to strip them of their authority often by the use of innuendos and murmuring. Ham's treatment of his father's nakedness is an example of the exposing nature of cynicism.

Pessimism is an attitude that expresses itself in the belief that *the evil in life outweighs the good*. It is the tendency to expect the worst outcomes. Leaders affected by pessimism have a disposition to finding the gloomiest possible view. "What is the worst case scenario?" they proclaim, pretending that they are simply being realistic or pragmatic. They tend to believe that Murphy's Law rather than Maxwell's Law applies in all circumstances. Murphy's Law notes that:

> Nothing is as easy as it looks; everything takes longer than you expect; and if anything can go wrong, it will and at the worst possible moment.

Maxwell's Law Notes that:

> Nothing is as hard as it looks; everything is more rewarding than you expect; and if anything can go right, it will and at the best possible moment.[4]

Adopting a negative framework is not being realistic, because it only sees the lack in any situation, instead of the abundance

---

[4] Maxwell. John Maxwell counters this Law with his own Law, which states:

of resources that can enable a group of people to take the next step towards achieving their goals or vision. Cynicism and pessimism produce attitudes of defeatism, despair, hopelessness and despondency in these leaders.

THE UNDERLYING SHEATH

Cynicism and pessimism produce in these leaders an invisible underlying sheath over their minds and hearts. This is an impervious barrier over their souls that prevent them from:

- Growing in maturity;[5] and

- Allowing the true purifying work of God's refining fire to have real effect in their souls.[6]

---

[5] **Paul writes in 1 Corinthians 3:1-3(NASB):** "And I, brethren, could not speak to you as to spiritual men, but as to men of flesh, as to infants in Christ. [2] I gave you milk to drink, not solid food; for you were not yet able to receive it. Indeed, even now you are not yet able, [3] for you are still fleshly. For since there is jealousy and strife among you, are you not fleshly, and are you not walking like mere men?"

The Letter to Hebrews 5:11-14 (NASB) notes: "Concerning him we have much to say, and it is hard to explain, since you have become dull of hearing. [12] For though by this time you ought to be teachers, you have need again for someone to teach you the elementary principles of the oracles of God, and you have come to need milk and not solid food. [13] For everyone who partakes only of milk is not accustomed to the word of righteousness, for he is an infant. [14] But solid food is for the mature, who because of practice have their senses trained to discern good and evil".

[6] **Malachi 3:1-3 (NASB):** "Behold, I am going to send My messenger, and he will clear the way before Me. And the Lord, whom you seek, will suddenly come to His temple; and the messenger of the covenant, in whom you delight, behold, He is coming," says the LORD of hosts. [2] "But who can endure the day of His coming? And who can stand when He appears? For He is like a refiner's fire and like fullers' soap. [3] He will sit as a smelter and purifier of silver, and He will purify the sons of Levi and refine them like gold and silver, so that they may present to the LORD offerings in righteousness".

They even pray for God's fire believing it to be some type of magical essence that transforms them without there being a change in their attitudes or behaviour. This is because they misunderstand the nature of that fire. God's refining fire comes in the form of trials and tribulations that test our faith, heart and attitudes to see whether we reflect a pure trust and faith in God. It tests our obedience to His will and purpose no matter what the circumstances might be. When we sing or pray for fire we are *asking* God to send trouble our way.

These leaders develop a resistance to hearing wise counsel and teaching from the leaders over them in the Lord. The outworking of cynicism and pessimism in their lives develops an autonomous attitude of heart and closes them off from sound direction and instruction from those leaders.[7] This underlying sheath of cynicism and pessimism produces:

- Defensive behaviour;

- An unteachable spirit;

- Unbelief;

- Stubbornness;

---

1 Corinthians 3:10-15 (NASB): "According to the grace of God which was given to me, like a wise master builder I laid a foundation, and another is building on it. But each man must be careful how he builds on it. [11] For no man can lay a foundation other than the one which is laid, which is Jesus Christ. [12] Now if any man builds on the foundation with gold, silver, precious stones, wood, hay, straw, [13] each man's work will become evident; for the day will show it because it is to be revealed with fire, and the fire itself will test the quality of each man's work. [14] If any man's work which he has built on it remains, he will receive a reward. [15] If any man's work is burned up, he will suffer loss; but he himself will be saved, yet so as through fire".

[7] Hebrews 13: 7, 17.

- An underlying murmuring and grumbling;

- Disloyalty;

- Mistrust – doubting other people's motives; and

- A depreciation of other people's skills and abilities.[8]

There are a number of biblical passages that describe the influence and effect of cynicism and pessimism on the community of faith. Paul and Jude often referred to the early church as being infected by elements that would destroy its unity, peace and effectiveness:

- Grumblers, malcontents, loudmouthed boasters (Jude 16 RSV);

- People who "bite and devour one another" (Galatians 5:15 RSV);

- Groups unbending in their contentiousness (1 Corinthians 1:10-17).

Paul warns us against involvement in godless chatter, and with people who are factious, and quarreling, jealousy, anger, selfishness, slander, gossip, conceit, and disorder.

---

[8] Peter Steinke compares such leaders and team members as anxiety viruses operating in the life of the church. He describes it as an intracellular parasite whose single purpose is the replicate itself. The characteristics of people with this virus are: can not say "no" to themselves; do not respect, or have, boundaries; cannot regulate themselves, go where they do not belong; have no ability to learn from their experiences; and cannot sacrifice for the sake of others. He notes that such people are like intracellular parasites with no life of their own. Peter Steinke, *Healthy Congregations, a System Approach* (New York: Alban Institute, 1996), 56.

Murmurings against the Lord and His servant Moses cost a generation of the Israelites their inheritance and destiny.[9] The despising the Lord's provision in hard and difficult situations, and a desire for the fleshpots of Egypt cost them their destiny.[10]

Luke and John use the word *goggizo* (which means to grumble, murmur, and speak complainingly against someone; to speak secretly or in a whisper) on several occasions to outline the attitude of the following different groups of people:

- The Jews, Pharisees and scribes murmuring against Jesus (Luke 15:2; John 6:41);

- Hellenists murmured against the Hebrews over the distribution of food to the widows (Acts 6:1); and

- The disciples murmuring against what Jesus had said (John 6:61).[11]

OVERCOMING CYNICISM & PESSIMISM

Any leader or team member who is going to be effective in his or her ministry needs to identify cynicism and pessimism as enemies that will rob him or her of that effectiveness. To overcome the corroding activity of cynicism and pessimism in our souls we need to:

- Recognise its presence in our soul;

- Repent of disbelief and its outworking;

---

[9] Exodus 16: 7; Numbers 14: 27.

[10] Exodus 17: 7; Numbers 21: 5.

[11] Steinke, 55.

- Ask God's forgiveness;

- Stand against it in the name of Jesus, rebuking the enemy and commanding him to yield the ground he has taken in our life; and

- Build new hope in our lives – the hope that does not disappoint – Romans 5:1-5.

The stance against cynicism and pessimism needs to be an ongoing activity in a leader's life and the team he or she leads. We need to challenge one another to move beyond the unbelief of such corrosive influences in our life, fighting the battle of faith to achieve the vision and goals that have been laid before us.

APPENDIX TWO - EXULT IN OUR TRIBULATIONS

Paul writes:

> Therefore, having been justified by faith, we have peace with God through our Lord Jesus Christ, [2] through whom also we have obtained our introduction by faith into this grace in which we stand; and we exult in hope of the glory of God. [3] And not only this, but we also exult in our tribulations, knowing that tribulation brings about perseverance; [4] and perseverance, proven character; and proven character, hope; [5] and hope does not disappoint, because the love of God has been poured out within our hearts through the Holy Spirit who was given to us (Romans 5:1-5 NASB).

EXULT IN OUR TRIBULATIONS

Thlipsis – Greek word **Θλιψις** (*thlipsis*) means pressure, compression, straightness – *hence* – pressure from evils, affliction, or distress. In modern terminology it is the type of trouble we refer to as **being between a rock and a hard place**. It is trouble that is not easily avoidable, insists on getting in our way and works to prevent us from doing the things God wants us to do.

In the Old and New Testaments this word is used in three ways:

1/ Justified affliction and trouble that are a result of us leaving God and His ways:

Deuteronomy 4:30 (NASB) - Moses warns the people that when they turn away from God and His ways they will meet with distress (which he graphically describes referring to the number of ills that will come their way). He then says:

> When you are in **distress** and all these things have come upon you, in the latter days you will return to the Lord your God and listen to His voice.

1 Samuel 10:19 (NASB): Samuel said, "But you have today rejected your God, who delivers you from all your calamities and your *distresses*; yet you have said, 'No, but set a king over us!' Now therefore, present yourselves before the Lord by your tribes and by your clans."

Nehemiah 9:36-37 (NASB) – Nehemiah notes the condition of the nation of Israel after they had returned from exile in Babylon when he addresses God with these words:

> Behold, we are slaves today, and as to the land which You gave to our fathers to eat of its fruit and its bounty, Behold, we are slaves in it. Its abundant produce is for the kings whom You have set over us because of our sins. They also rule over our bodies and over our cattle as they please, so we are in great **distress**.

Isaiah 8:19-22 (NASB) - Isaiah warns of the percussions of involving ourselves in New Age and Occult practices. Repercussion that will leave them without hope and the land:

> When they say to you, 'Consult the mediums and the spiritists who whisper and mutter,' should not a people consult their God? Should they consult the dead on behalf of the living? To the law and to the testimony! If they do not speak according to this word, it is because they have no dawn. They will pass through the land hard-pressed and famished, and it will turn out that when they are hungry, they will be enraged and curse their king and their God as they face upward. Then they will look to the

earth, and behold, **distress** and darkness, the gloom of anguish; and they will be driven away into darkness".

Paul uses it also in this sense in:

Romans 2:9-10 (NASB) – "There will be tribulation and **distress** for every soul of man who does evil, of the Jew first and also of the Greek, but glory and honor and peace to everyone who does good, to the Jew first and also to the Greek".

Jesus uses the term to refer to the great tribulation coming upon the whole world a number of times.

Mark 13:19 (NASB) – "For those days will be a time of **tribulation** such as has not occurred since the beginning of the creation which God created until now, and never will" (see also Matthew 24:20-21,29).

John also uses in the sense of the great tribulation when he writes

Revelation 7:14 (NASB) – "I said to him, 'My lord, you know.' And he said to me, 'These are the ones who come out of the great **tribulation**, and they have washed their robes and made them white in the blood of the Lamb'" (see also Revelation 1:9).

2/ Unjustified affliction and trouble that have come because we belong to God, are committed to His purpose and aim to live in righteousness.

Psalm 119:142-143 (NASB): "Your righteousness is an ever-lasting righteousness, and Your law is truth. **Trouble** and anguish have come upon me, yet Your commandments are my delight".

Matthew 24:9 (NASB) - "Then they will deliver you to **tribulation**, and will kill you, and you will be hated by all nations because of My name".

1 Thessalonians 1:6-7 (NASB) – "You also became imitators of us and of the Lord, having received the word in much **tribulation** with the joy of the Holy Spirit, so that you became an example to all the believers in Macedonia and in Achaia".

2 Corinthians 1:3-4, 8-9 (NASB) – "Blessed be the God and Father of our Lord Jesus Christ, the Father of mercies and God of all comfort, who comforts us in all our affliction so that we will be able to comfort those who are in any affliction with the comfort with which we ourselves are comforted by God"... 8-9 "For we do not want you to be unaware, brethren, of our affliction which came to us in Asia, that we were burdened excessively, beyond our strength, so that we despaired even of life; indeed, we had the sentence of death within ourselves so that we would not trust in ourselves, but in God who raises the dead".

3/ Refers to the transforming process of God in our lives to strengthen our character and develop our personality.

In Romans 5:3 the term still carries with it that unjustified affliction and trouble that have come because we belong to God, are committed to His purpose and aim to live in righteousness. It also includes the immense stresses that life brings to us from time to time that tempt us to flee from God's presence and purpose and become bitter, resentful and critical in our lives.

Paul, as we noted, understands what it means to be between a rock and a hard place. Yet he still has the effrontery to tell us to rejoice at the coming of such problems and difficulties. Rather, he goes further than that and tells us to exult in them. Paul's history in his relationship with God notes that we should not exult in anything but the Lord Jesus Christ. But here he tells us to exult in them because we need to position ourselves properly to handle them. We need to approach these troubles, difficulties, afflictions, persecution or other similar things in such a way that we make use of them for our benefit, rather than them wiping us out. Because when we wipe out, we lose all hope in the world.

Our response to these difficulties can produce an unbelievable hope and expectation that will see miraculous things happen around us. This comes because we have allowed these situations to develop us as people of character. Paul tells:

> We know that tribulation brings about perseverance; and perseverance, proven character; and proven character, hope, and hope does not disappoint, because the love of God has been poured out within our hearts through the Holy Spirit who was given to us (Romans 5:4-5 NASB).

I think it a moot point to ask whether we have encountered any troubles or difficulties in recent time, that we could call being between a rock and a hard place. Our own church and individuals have encounter numerous instances when faith was the only thing left and the only course of action was to persevere, doggedly going forward despite the circumstances.

However, we each need to reflect on these questions:

- Have we prospered from our tribulations or have they weighed us down or for some brought us down?

- Have we grown in character over the last five years; or in an attempt to avoid tribulation, have we compromised ourselves?

- Have we sought an unrealisable hope or are we focused on a hope that will not disappoint?

Growing in Times of Tribulation

There are four things that help us to grow in times when tribulation is so strong that we are literally between a rock and a hard place:

- **Giving:** Jesus said – "Give, and it will be given to you. They will pour into your lap a good measure—pressed down, shaken together, and running over. For by your standard of measure it will be measured to you in return" (Luke 6:38 NASB).

- **Peace:** Jesus said – "Peace I leave with you; My peace I give to you; not as the world gives do I give to you. Do not let your heart be troubled, nor let it be fearful" (John 14:27-28 NASB).

- **Love:** Jesus said - "This is My commandment, that you love one another, just as I have loved you. [13] Greater love has no one than this, that one lay down his life for his friends (John 15:12-13 NASB).

- **Prayer:** Jesus said - "Ask, and it will be given to you; seek, and you will find; knock, and it will be opened to you. For everyone who asks receives, and he who seeks finds, and to him who knocks it will be opened" (Matthew7:7-8 NASB).

A fully perfected or mature person of God (saint) – needs to serve or else he or she becomes bloated. Christianity is an action centred faith – we are called to bear fruit in addition to being loveable and adorable persons.

There are three things God wants to develop in our lives:

1. A Christian life that reflects the presence of Jesus Christ in our life;[1]

2. A Ministry development that enables us to serve God effectively in the things He has called to do and to bear fruit; and

3. A leadership development that enables us to assist others to grow and develop and Christian men, women and children.

PASSAGES USING *THLIPSIS* IN NEW TESTAMENT

PERSEVERANCE IN TRIBULATION:

Matthew 13:21 (NASB): Jesus said, "The one on whom seed was sown on the rocky places, this is the man who hears the word and immediately receives it with joy; [21] yet he has no firm root in himself, but is only temporary, and when affliction or persecution arises because of the word, immediately he falls away".

Romans 8:35-37 (NASB): "[35] who will separate us from the love of Christ? Will tribulation, or distress, or persecution, or famine, or nakedness, or peril, or sword?

---

[1] Two attributes especially note this reflection: 1/ A peace that passes all understanding: its purpose is not to comfort us as you would think. Rather, its purpose is to enable us to stay focused on the purpose of God and His Kingdom no matter what trouble surrounds us; and 2/ A friend giving up His life for His friends: this is what Jesus did so we could have the ability to love one another.

36 Just as it is written, "For Your sake we are being put to death all day long; we were considered as sheep to be slaughtered." 37 But in all these things we overwhelmingly conquer through Him who loved us".

Romans 12:12 (NASB): "9 Let love be without hypocrisy. Abhor what is evil; cling to what is good. 10 Be devoted to one another in brotherly love; give preference to one another in honor; 11 not lagging behind in diligence, fervent in spirit, serving the Lord; 12 rejoicing in hope, persevering in tribulation, devoted to prayer, 13 contributing to the needs of the saints, practicing hospitality".

Ephesians 3:13 (NASB): "11 This was in accordance with the eternal purpose which He carried out in Christ Jesus our Lord, 12 in whom we have boldness and confident access through faith in Him. 13 Therefore I ask you not to lose heart at my tribulations on your behalf, for they are your glory".

Acts 14:22 (NASB): "21 After they had preached the gospel to that city and had made many disciples, they returned to Lystra and to Iconium and to Antioch, 22 strengthening the souls of the disciples, encouraging them to continue in the faith, and saying, "Through many tribulations we must enter the kingdom of God."

Romans 5:3 (NASB): "3 And not only this, but we also exult in our tribulations, knowing that tribulation brings about perseverance".

1 Thessalonians 1:4,6 (NASB): 4 therefore, we ourselves speak proudly of you among the churches of God for your perseverance and faith in the midst of all your persecutions and afflictions which you endure. 5 This is a plain indication of God's righteous judgment so that you will be considered worthy of the kingdom of God, for which indeed you are suffering. 6 For after all it is only just for God to repay with affliction those who afflict you".

Revelation 2:9, 10, 22 (NASB): "9 'I know your tribulation and your poverty (but you are rich), and the blasphemy by those who say they are Jews and are not, but are a synagogue of Satan. 10 Do not fear what you are about to suffer. Behold, the devil is about to cast some of you into prison, so that you will be tested, and you will have tribulation for ten days. Be faithful until death, and I will give you the crown of life. 11 He who has an ear, let him hear what the Spirit says to the churches. He who overcomes will not be hurt by the second death.' Behold, I will throw her on a bed of sickness, and those who commit adultery with her into great tribulation, unless they repent of her deeds".

AFFLICTION OR DISTRESS:

Mark 4:17 (NASB): "and they have no firm root in themselves, but are only temporary; then, when affliction or persecution arises because of the word, immediately they fall away".

Acts 7:10, 11 (NASB): 9 "The patriarchs became jealous of Joseph and sold him into Egypt. Yet God was with him, 10 and rescued him from all his afflictions, and granted him favor and wisdom in the sight of Pharaoh, king of Egypt, and he made him governor over Egypt and all his household. 11 "Now a famine came over all Egypt and Canaan, and great affliction with it, and our fathers could find no food".

Acts 20:23 (NASB): "22 And now, behold, bound by the Spirit, I am on my way to Jerusalem, not knowing what will happen to me there, 23 except that the Holy Spirit solemnly testifies to me in every city, saying that bonds and afflictions await me".

Colossians 1:24 (NASB): "[24] Now I rejoice in my sufferings for your sake, and in my flesh I do my share on behalf of His body, which is the church, in filling up what is lacking in Christ's afflictions".

Colossians 3:3,7 (NASB): "[6] But now that Timothy has come to us from you, and has brought us good news of your faith and love, and that you always think kindly of us, longing to see us just as we also long to see you, [7] for this reason, brethren, in all our distress and affliction we were comforted about you through your faith; 8 for now we really live, if you stand firm in the Lord".

Philippians 1:16 (NASB): "[15] Some, to be sure, are preaching Christ even from envy and strife, but some also from good will; [16] the latter do it out of love, knowing that I am appointed for the defense of the gospel; [17] the former proclaim Christ out of selfish ambition rather than from pure motives, thinking to cause me distress in my imprisonment".

Hebrews 10:33 (NASB): "[32] But remember the former days, when, after being enlightened, you endured a great conflict of sufferings, [33] partly by being made a public spectacle through reproaches and tribulations, and partly by becoming sharers with those who were so treated. [34] For you showed sympathy to the prisoners and accepted joyfully the seizure of your property, knowing that you have for yourselves a better possession and a lasting one. [35] Therefore, do not throw away your confidence, which has a great reward".

Hebrews 11:25 (NASB): "[24] By faith Moses, when he had grown up, refused to be called the son of Pharaoh's daughter, [25] choosing rather to endure ill-treatment with the people of God than to enjoy the passing pleasures of sin, [26] considering the reproach of Christ greater riches than the treasures of Egypt; for he was looking to the reward".

James 1:27 (NASB): "[27] Pure and undefiled religion in the sight of our God and Father is this: to visit orphans and widows in their distress, and to keep oneself unstained by the world".

TROUBLE

1 Corinthians 7:28 (NASB): "[28] But if you marry, you have not sinned; and if a virgin marries, she has not sinned. Yet such will have trouble in this life, and I am trying to spare you".

ANGUISH

John 16:21 (NASB): "[20] Truly, truly, I say to you, that you will weep and lament, but the world will rejoice; you will grieve, but your grief will be turned into joy. [21] Whenever a woman is in labor she has pain, because her hour has come; but when she gives birth to the child, she no longer remembers the anguish because of the joy that a child has been born into the world. [22] Therefore you too have grief now; but I will see you again, and your heart will rejoice, and no one will take your joy away from you".

BURDENED

2 Corinthians 8:13 (NASB): "[12] For if the readiness is present, it is acceptable according to what a person has, not according to what he does not have. [13] For this is not for the ease of others and for your affliction, but by way of equality— [14] at this present time your abundance being a supply for their need, so that their abundance also may become a supply for your need, that there may be equality; [15] as it is written, "He who gathered much did not have too much, and he who gathered little had no lack."

Bibliography:

Alexander, T. Desmond, and Brian Rosner. "New Dictionary of Biblical Theology." (2001).

Bromiley, Geoffrey. *Theological Dictionary of the New Testament.* Grand Rapids, Michigan: William B Eerdmans Publishing Co, 1985.

Brown, Colin, ed. *The New International Dictionary of New Testament Theology.* Vol. 3. Devon: The Paternoster Press, 1986.

Brown, Raymond, Joseph Fitzmeyer, and Roland Murphy. *The New Jerome Biblical Commentary.* New Jersey: Geoffrey Chapman, 1990.

Bullinger, E. W. *A Critical Lexicon and Concordance.* London: Samuel Bagster and Sons Limited, 1971.

Cranfield, C.E.B. *A Critical and Exegetical Commentary on the Epistle to the Romans.* Edinburgh: T & TClark Ltd, 1975.

Ferguson, Sinclair B., and David F Wright. *New Dictionary of Theology.* Downers, Grove, IL: InterVarsity Press, 2000, c1988.

Gadamer, Hans. *Truth and Method.* New York: Crossroad, 1992.

Gorringe, Tim. *God's Theatre: A Theology of Providence*. London: SCM Press, 1991.

Hersey, P, K Blanchard, and D Johnson. *Management of Organizational Behavior*. Upper Saddle River, NJ: Prentice Hall, 1996.

Houston, Brian. *Get a Life*. Sydney: Hillsong, 1996.

Kurian, G.T. *Nelson's New Christian Dictionary*. Nashville: Thomas Nelson Publishers, 2001.

Martin, Ralph. *2 Corinthians* Word Biblical Commentary, Edited by David Hubbard, Glenn Barker and Ralph Martin. Milton Keynes: Word Publishing, 1986, 1991.

Maxwell, John. *The Winning Attitude*.

Moltmann, Jürgen. *Ethics of Hope*. Translated by Margaret Kohl. London: SCM Press, 2012.

Parsons, George, and Speed B. Leas. *Understanding Your Congregation as a System*. New York: Alban Institute Publications, 1994.

Peters, Andrew. *The Emerging Paradigm of Diversity*. Mansfield, QLD: A.E. & L.A. Peters Outreach Enterprises, 2011.

Saucy, Robert. *Scripture: Its Power, Authority and Relevance*. Nashville: Word Publishing, 2001.

Steinke, Peter. *Healthy Congregations, a System Approach*. New York: Alban Institute, 1996.

Treier, Daniel. *Proverbs & Ecclesiastes*. Grand Rapids, MI: Brazos Press, 2011.

Weinsheimer, Joel. *Gadamer's Hermeneutics, a Reading of Truth and Method*. New Haven: Yale University Press, 1985.